DoubleBlue

Double Blue

Edited by
Jim O'Leary
and
Wayne Parrish

ECW PRESS

Toronto Argonauts Football Club
Rogers Centre, 1 Blue Jays Way, Suite 3300, Toronto, Ontario, Canada M5V 1J3
www.argonauts.ca

Published by ECW Press
2120 Queen Street East, Suite 200, Toronto, Ontario, Canada M4E 1E2
www.ecwpress.com

Produced by Sport Media Publishing
55 Mill Street, Building 5, Suite 240, Toronto, Ontario, Canada M5A 3C4
www.sportclassicbooks.com

Library and Archives Canada Cataloguing in Publication

Double Blue : an illustrated history of the Toronto Argonauts / Wayne Parrish, editor.

ISBN 978-1-55022-779-6

1. Toronto Argonauts (Football team)—History. I. Parrish, Wayne, 1955-

GV948.3.T67D69 2007 796.335'6409713541 C2006-906832-1

This book is set in Mrs. Eaves, Gill Sans and Tanek.

Cover design: Paul Hodgson
Interior design: Paul Hodgson and Greg Oliver
Printing: Transcontinental

The publication of *Double Blue* has been generously supported by the Book Publishing Industry Development Program.

DISTRIBUTION
Canada: Jaguar Book Group, 100 Armstrong Ave., Georgetown, ON L7G 5S4
United States: Independent Publishers Group, 814 North Franklin St., Chicago, Ill., 60610

Printed and bound in Canada

ECW PRESS
ecwpress.com

Table of Contents

Introduction

As we enter our fourth season as co-owners of your Toronto Argonauts, we wanted to create a special book, a personal book, complete with stories from fans, alumni and family to capture and cherish key moments in the history of this storied franchise. We purchased the Double Blue out of receivership in November 2003. We attended the East Final in Montreal and watched the team lose in what has gone down in history as a controversial call. We didn't know at that point how personal wins and losses would become to us. Our families did not yet know that we would be unable to hold a conversation during a game and our friends could not yet comprehend how upset we would become at each game the Argos would lose and how ecstatic we would be at each win.

We had come to the Double Blue as huge CFL fans. Howard grew up in Toronto and had been an Argo season ticket holder for years, following the history and stats. David had grown up in Edmonton where he sold hot dogs at the Eskimos games. He had gone on to play football at York University. Former CFL Commissioner Tom Wright brought the two of us together to own and operate this club. We knew we had been entrusted with an integral part of Toronto's sporting history and tradition and wanted to see it thrive. We live in Toronto so it is personal to us, just like it is personal to you, our fans.

Winning the Grey Cup in 2004, our rookie season as owners, was an unbelievable experience. Being on the field as the Mounties brought in

I met the owners for the first time at the East Final in Montreal in 2003. They walked right up to me, shook my hand and said 'Hi, Jude!' It took me aback—it was so different from before. The fact that they had just bought the team and already knew me by name showed me how passionate they were about the Argos.

Jude St. John, *long-time Argos guard*

the Cup and being presented with it, with the great energy around us, was overwhelming. We still dream of that perfect night—a night made complete by the people working with us: President and CEO Keith Pelley, General Manager Adam Rita, Head Coach Pinball Clemons and the Argo players who put it all on the line that night in Ottawa.

This year, we cannot wait to bring the Argo faithful the Grey Cup at home in Toronto for the first time in fifteen years. It has been too long but we believe football and the Argonauts are now firmly entrenched in Toronto. We are looking forward to seeing the crowds at the game and the festival where we will show the entire country what the CFL and the Argonauts mean to our city. Seeing more and more people in the stands each season shows us how far we have come thanks to your support.

Please enjoy this trip down memory lane. We grew up idolizing Warren Moon, Condredge Holloway, Hank Ilesic and the Gold Dust Twins. The excitement and entertainment provided by this game that we love is second to none. We thank you for bringing a new generation of kids to the games so that they can idolize and get to know Damon Allen, Orlondo Steinauer, Noel Prefontaine and Michael Fletcher, the stars of today. Not only do we thrive watching these players pull together on the field in the quest for another championship, their commitment to our greater Toronto community is second to none and for that, we are forever rewarded by our experience as the owners of your Toronto Argonauts.

See you on the field!

David Cynamon and Howard Sokolowski

The owners can be described as the three C's—they're connected, committed and Canadian.

Keith Pelley,
President & CEO

Right David Cynamon.
Far right Howard Sokolowski.

The Argos Today

The Toronto Argonauts are as proud of their past as they are excited about their future. Every club initiative since 2004 has been guided by the 22 simple words that comprise the Argonauts mission statement: *To be Toronto's ultimate role model, setting the standard by combining a competitive spirit, great entertainment value and community involvement and pride.*

Those words are to the Argos what air is to a football, and have laid the foundation for triumph on the field and success in the community. From the executive suites to the coaches' offices to the players' clubhouse, the entire organization shares a commitment to Toronto, as evidenced by the vignettes here from six Argo stalwarts.

CHAD FOLK, CENTRE, TEAM CO-CAPTAIN
After moving here from B.C., it was evident that this was the place that I would soon call home. The community and the relationship we have with the people of Toronto is almost like none that I have ever experienced before. It is for that reason that my wife and I have decided to make Toronto our home. In addition, although ownership has changed over the years, there has always been that steady nucleus of guys like O'Shea, Pre and Jude.

ADAM RITA, **GM AND VP, FOOTBALL OPERATIONS**
The thing that stands out to me about the fans has been their dedication. A lot of our more loyal fans I remember being with us in 1991 when we had Rocket and all those guys. They are still with us today and that is great to see. A lot of that has to do with the organization which has grown over the years as well as the community around it.

ORLONDO STEINAUER, SAFETY

The Argonauts' renewed commitment to the community has allowed me the opportunity to be involved with my passion ... people! It has also reinforced that together we all can make a difference.

ANDRE TALBOT, **RECEIVER**

My most memorable moment as an Argo is, without a doubt, winning the Grey Cup in 2004. It was an incredible experience that I will remember forever. There are many other great memories from "on the field" that I recall since becoming an Argo in 2001, but some of the most uplifting moments were those spent talking to kids at the various schools across the GTA that we visit and all the great fans that I have met over the years.

TONY MILES, RECEIVER

David and Howard's ownership has made the Argonauts one of the most recognizable teams in the city through community involvement and other programs. They have made Toronto a destination that many of the top-tier players in the CFL want to come and be a part of. They are also people owners. They are always around and they listen to the players and the fans. They have helped to build a family atmosphere.

CHUCK WINTERS, **LINEBACKER**

The Argonauts organization and the fans have had a profound effect on me and my family. The quintessential part of this equation is the fans. They never fail to open their arms and hearts to me and make me feel very thankful for being a member of the oldest and greatest football team in North America.

Far left Chuck Winters and Adrion "Pee Wee" Smith sign autographs, 2006.

Middle Andre Talbot and the Blue Thunder Cheerleaders at Easter Seals Telethon, 2006.

Far right Argos owners David Cynamon and Howard Sokolowski, and President & CEO Keith Pelley display the Grey Cup at Toronto's City Hall, 2004.

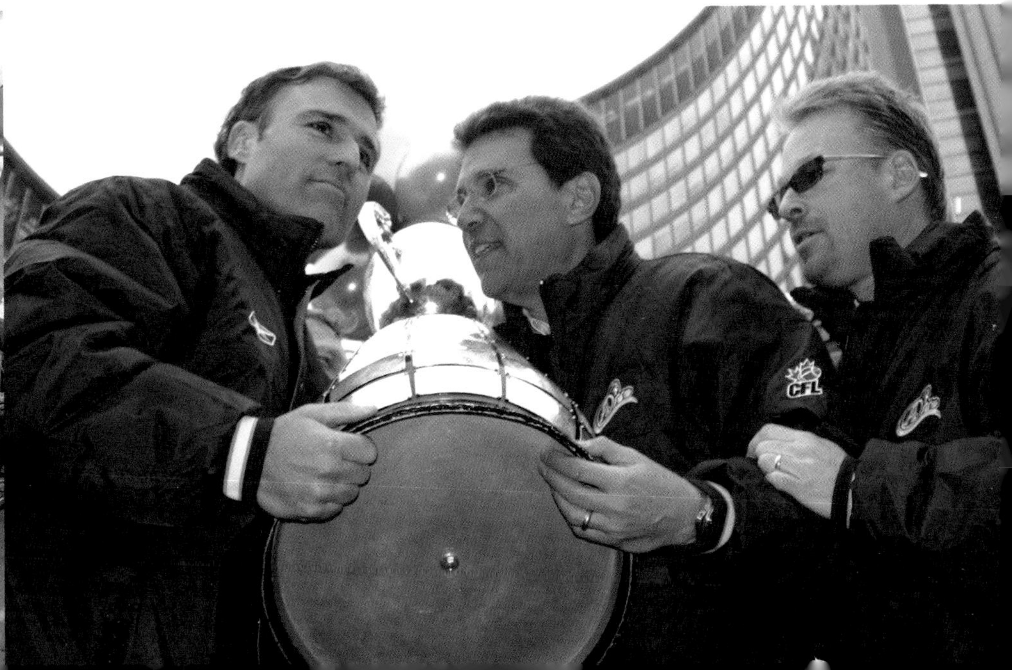

SECTION I

1

The Argo Bounce

The year was 1949 and Annis Stukus, a two-time Grey Cup champion with the Toronto Argonauts, had gone west to become the general

manager and coach of the Edmonton Eskimos. An easterner, he had to speak a language that would resonate in the west. So he promised Edmonton fans that if they looked between the lines of his Eskimos' playbook they'd find the most famous football ploy in the country.

He promised them the Argo Bounce.

Literally speaking, of course, that wasn't a promise Stukus could keep. The Argo Bounce wasn't something to be X'ed and O'ed in a playbook. Nor executed at will. That was part of its appeal. Many die-hard football fans would be baffled by the detail of any playbook, but by 1949 they all knew the Argo Bounce.

"We'll use a lot of Argo plays," Stukus said during a barnstorming promotional tour in March of that year. And maybe as quick as he spoke those words he realized his fumble because he laughed and quickly added, "We'll even put the Argo Bounce to good use."

The Argo Bounce. If the term were to be found in the *Canadian Encyclopedia* it might be defined as follows: *Originally, an uncanny stroke of good fortune that often, but not necessarily, involved a dropped or loose football taking an unexpected and peculiar change of direction to land in the hands of a waiting Toronto Argonaut football player at a key moment in an important game, leaving opposing coaches, players and fans stupefied. Today, the term can be applied more broadly to any bizarre bounce or game-altering event that bestows an astonishing change of fortune upon one team or the other.*

The historical record shows that Stukus often referred to the Argo Bounce. He may have coined the phrase or maybe not. If it wasn't Stukus

Left Argos running back Gil Fenerty loses his grip against the Ticats, 1987.

Previous page Following the bouncing ball versus Ottawa Rough Riders, 1981.

it might have been an unhappy opposing coach or one of his players after an unfathomable loss to the Argos. Or maybe a relieved Argos' coach or player after a lucky win. Who knows? No account has surfaced of a single event or utterance that planted the seed for this rose of football expression.

It was most certainly born sometime in the 1930s, but when? Some point to the 1937 Grey Cup game, a 4-3 Argos' victory over Winnipeg. Others will tell you it arrived with the Argos' 30-7 win over the Blue Bombers in the 1938 Grey Cup. But the origins of the Bounce might be traced as far back as 1933.

"It started with Lew Hayman," recalled Don Durno, an Argo in 1948, '49 and '51. "I don't remember exactly when but I know it started after Hayman arrived."

Hayman left Syracuse to join the huddle of Canadian football in 1933 and stayed for 48 years as a coach, executive and owner. He won his first of five Grey Cups—the first coach to win five times—in his rookie season as the Argos beat the Sarnia Imperials 4-3. None of the post-game writeups mention the Argo Bounce specifically. But you don't have to strain your eyes to spot the Bounce. It appeared under a nom de plume.

Sarnia was the better team that day. As Lou Marsh (a former Argo) wrote in the *Toronto Star*, "Sarnia had the edge in forward passing, broken-field running and general all-round tackling." The Cup would have been theirs, wrote Marsh, "but Miss Ill Luck cut them out of what looked like a sure touchdown and the all-Dominion title."

Below Lew Hayman works with Tobin Rote, 1960.

Miss Ill Luck (aka Argo Bounce) arrived with the score tied 3-3 and Sarnia the popular choice to succeed. But then Sarnia's Alex Hayes, their most reliable ball handler, tripped up on a punt return and saw the ball squirt into the hands of the Argos' Jim Palmer. That's the thing about the Argo Bounce. For Argo foes, its arrival is unpredictable, its outcome calamitous. Hayes' fumble set up a single by Argo kicker Ab Box to put Toronto ahead 4-3. Another characteristic of the Argo Bounce is that it is relentless. On the ensuing drive, Sarnia's Norman Perry took a pass at mid-field and broke down the sideline with nothing between him and

If there had not been an honest official on duty, (the) Argos would not be champions today

the endzone but 50 or so yards of frozen turf. He was within two strides of a game-winning touchdown when Box, from well behind, dove frantically and, with one hand, managed to clip Perry's back heel. It was a one-in-a-hundred shot. Perry stumbled off stride and, six inches from glory, official Jo-Jo Stirrett thought he saw Perry step out of bounds before Perry lurched desperately over the goal line. There was, of course, no replay to refute the blink-of-an-eye call, so Perry's apparent touchdown was disallowed and the Argos were presented their third Grey Cup.

"If there had not been an honest official on duty, (the) Argos would not be champions today," concluded Marsh.

So maybe that was the day the Argo Bounce was born. There is no reason to suspect it was any earlier. From their formation in 1873 the Argos had no more or no less good fortune than any of the clubs that, over the decades, transformed the British game of rugby into the unique game of Canadian football. Even when the Argos won their first Grey Cup in 1914, beating the University of Toronto 14-2 (and scoring their only two touchdowns directly from fumble recoveries!) no eyebrows were raised. Their second Grey Cup triumph was a 23-0 drubbing of the Edmonton Eskimos in the first ever East-West final in 1921. The Argos got by just fine without a Bounce in that one. They had Lionel Conacher. Who needs an Argo Bounce when you have a Big Train?

From Conacher in 1921 through 1952, the Argos went to nine Grey Cup finals and won nine times. It would be silly, of course, to attribute that success to the Argo Bounce. The Argos consistently attracted many of the best athletes of that era. A trademark of great teams is an ability to make its breaks and then capitalize on them. The Argos had a knack for doing that. At least, that's how they saw it.

"Don't think the Argo Bounce is all about luck—it isn't," Annis Stukus once said. "Those boys chase the ball so much they actually end up knowing where it's going to bounce."

Charlie Camilleri won championships with the Argos in 1946 and '47. "Did we believe in the Argo Bounce? Of course we believed in it," he said

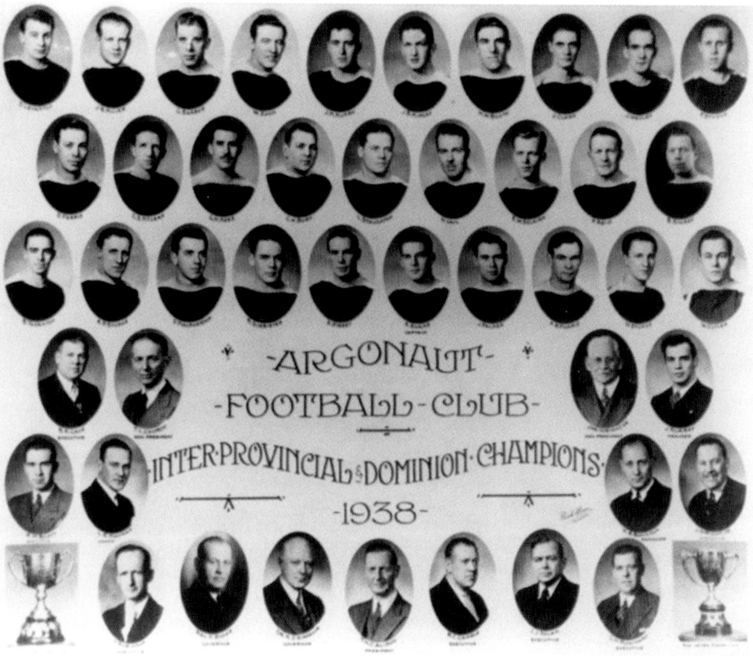

recently. "But we also believed we could make the bounce happen when we needed one."

But we're getting ahead of ourselves. The legend of the Argo Bounce was cemented long before 1947. Back-to-back championships in 1937 and '38 saw to that.

In 1937, the Argos beat Winnipeg 4-3 in an error-filled game in frigid conditions on a frozen Varsity Stadium field. The teams were as butter-fingered—there were nine fumbles in total—as they were stumble-footed when it came to capitalizing on chances. But in the end, the game turned on a call by an official from Winnipeg. The westerner, Eddie Grant, disallowed an apparent Bombers touchdown by Bill Ceretti who had scooped up the ball after Bill Stukus fumbled a punt return. Grant called a no-yards penalty on the Bombers and returned the ball to the Argos.

But was it no yards? Ted Reeve, writing in the *Toronto Telegram*, didn't think so. "He (Stukus) was given about as fair a chance to catch as is usually the case under this very elastic rule."

Grant was never forgiven in Winnipeg and soon afterwards moved to St. Thomas, Ontario, a victim of the Argo Bounce.

For some, the Argo Bounce was born in 1937 and fully christened late in the third quarter of the 1938 Grey Cup. The Bombers led 7-5 and, again, appeared to be the stronger team. "I believe the feeling was that at last the Argos had met their match," Lionel Conacher wrote in the *Toronto Star*. Then came the Bounce. Winnipeg's Ceretti blocked a Bob Isbister punt at midfield and saw teammate Bud Marquardt start booting the ball along the ground towards the end zone, where he intended to fall on it for a touchdown. He made it to the Argo nine and then the ball took a strange hop and was delivered into the hands of Argo sparkplug Teddy Morris. With that one strange bounce, agreed the experts, the game changed. Rather than take a comfortable lead into the fourth quarter, the Bombers saw the Argos come alive and roll to a 30-7 win.

Annis Stukus played on the 1937 and '38 champions, and after he retired he helped popularize the Argo Bounce in his newspaper writings in the 1940s. In one 1947 column he chided a pair of Hamilton punt returners for letting an Argo punt hit the ground before attempting to field it. Of course, wrote Stukus, the ball bounced crazily over their heads and through the end zone to hand the Argos the winning point on the game's final play. "One was too young to know about the Argo bounce and Stephens is an American import," Stukus sniffed. "Otherwise they'd never have given the ball the opportunity to bounce as it did."

By 1950 the Bounce was part of the everyday vernacular. Prior to the infamous Mud Bowl, Winnipeg coach Frank Larson predicted a wide-open game, "barring injuries and the famed Argo Bounce." And in 1952, prior to the West final, Winnipeg coach George Trafton believed the Eskimos and Bombers were so evenly matched the game would come down to whichever team got the "Argo Bounce." Skip forward now to the 1968 Grey Cup between Ottawa and Calgary at the old CNE. Riders' speedster Vic Washington took a pitch from Russ Jackson and, on his first step towards a 79-yard touchdown run, dropped the ball only to have it bounce miraculously back into his hands. He didn't miss a step. "It's the Toronto field," chuckled Ron Stewart, "the old Argo Bounce is still there."

If so, though, the Bounce wasn't there very often for the Argos during a 31-year dry spell that followed the 1952 Grey Cup. In fact, things got so bad for the Argos during the '50s, '60s and '70s that their plight prompted a book in 1981 ironically titled *The Argo Bounce.* Author Jay Teitel suggested that

Below Annis Stukus, the Loquacious Lithuanian, 1935-41.

the true meaning of Argo Bounce was lost to an entire generation of fans. To baby boomers, he said, the Argo Bounce "was the unluckiest bounce in the world, the one that usually arose from the Argos' uncanny ability to lose critical games in the dying minutes by committing an improbable blunder."

Teitel provided ample evidence, but none more convincing than the woes that befell the Argos in the dying minutes of the 1971 Grey Cup. Of course, that was the year Leon McQuay fumbled away a championship on the Calgary 10-yard line and Harry Abofs booted a punt return out of bounds in the dying seconds, thereby giving possession to the Stampeders by virtue of an obscure rule. Call it the Argo anti-Bounce.

Argo fortunes remained dismal for the next decade. Then at the 1983 Grey Cup the Argo Bounce returned. Trailing B.C. 17-12 late in the fourth quarter, Argos quarterback Joe Barnes threw to Paul Pearson at the Lions' 45. The ball squirted loose and, improbably, right into the hands of Toronto's Emmanuel Tolbert, keeping alive a drive that ended with a game-winning touchdown pass from Barnes to Cedric Minter. It was the Argos' first Cup since 1952.

In some ways, the Argo Bounce is like Argo history itself. It can be cruel or kind, funny or sad, failed or triumphant—always unpredictable. If you dig just a little bit you find it running like a thread to connect the many chapters of the long and celebrated story of the Toronto Argonauts.

~ Jim O'Leary

Right The ball squirts free from the grip of running back Leon McQuay — and the Grey Cup from the grasp of the Argonauts — on the wet turf of Vancouver's Empire Stadium in the 1971 Grey Cup game.

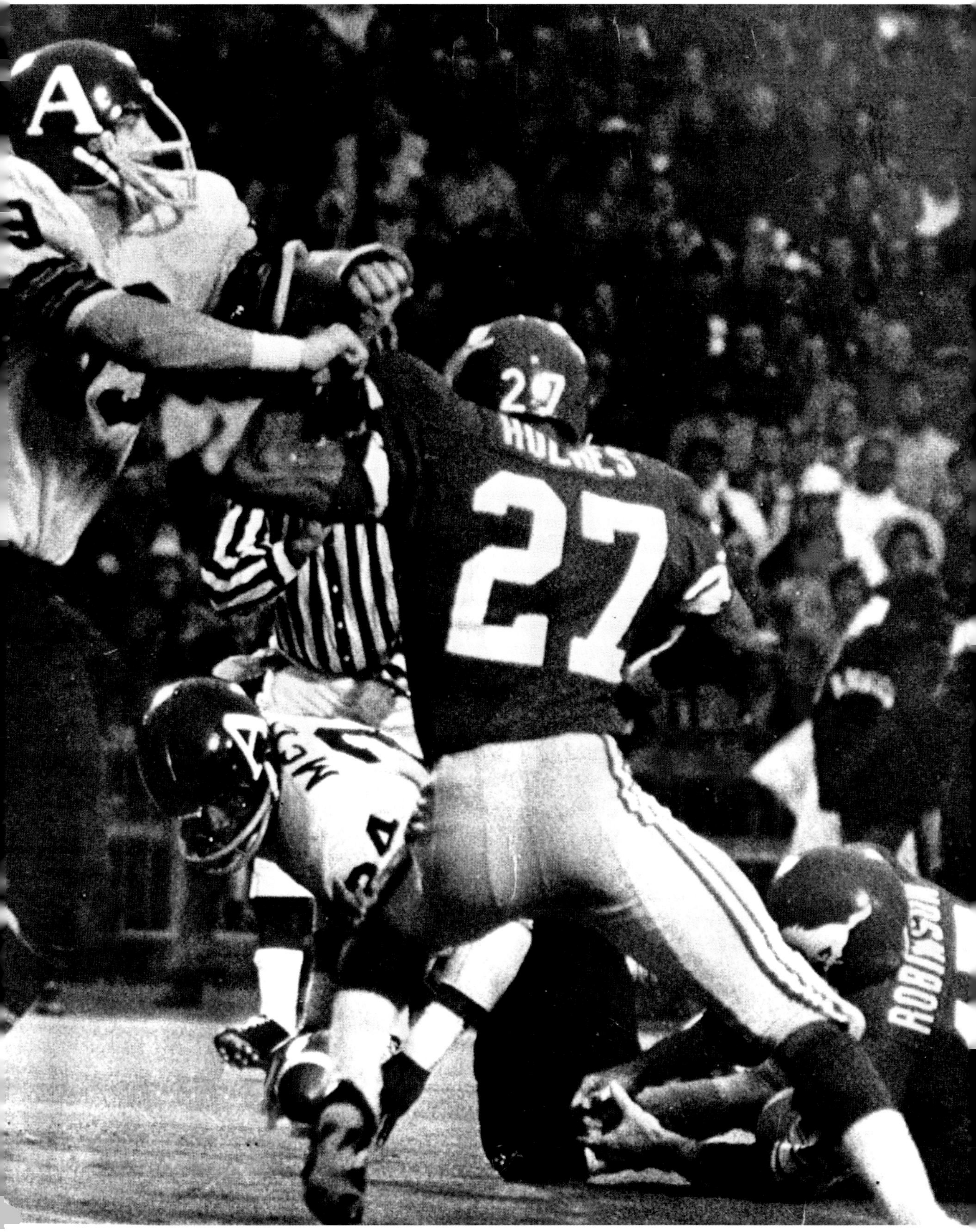
HOLMES
27
ROBINSON

Coming of Age

1873–1920

SECTION 2

CHALLENGE.

Fifteen of the New Dominion Rowing Club will

KICK A FRIENDLY MATCH OF FOOTBALL

With the same number of the Argonauts, on any Saturday that will suit them, Saturday 22nd preferred.

G. M. DONNELLY,
Sec. N. D. R. C.

HAMILTON VS. ARGONAUTS

ADMIT BEARER TO 'VARSITY GROUNDS GRAND STAND

SATURDAY, NOV. 12th, 1895

ADMISSION, 35 CENTS

No. 324

Above
The Argonauts' inaugural road game occurred in 1874 when a joint Toronto-Hamilton team played a Quebec team at the Montreal Cricket Grounds. This is a composite image of individual photos of the Ontario team superimposed at the time over an oil painting of the grounds with Mount Royal in the background.

Previous page
Jack Newton, 1912.

It was a practical beginning. In 1873, members of the Toronto Argonaut Rowing Club needed an

autumn pastime to keep them fit after their boats had been lifted from chilly Lake Ontario and put into winter storage. Organized professional sport did not exist, and the first Grey Cup game was still 36 years away. These earliest Argonauts were not visionaries. They did not set out to establish a game that would become a Canadian cultural institution. No, the earliest Argonauts were oarsmen who sought off-season exercise and competition.

So the "manly activity" of football was added to the rowing club's program solely to complement the club's primary mission of rowing. None would have suspected what was to follow. The game of football was entering a phase of growth, experimentation and evolution. Coming years would bring disagreement between those seeking to safeguard the traditional flavour of English rugby football and those seeking to introduce exciting modifications to the rules that were being championed in the United States. Today, we'd regard the outcome as a "typically Canadian" compromise, but in the last quarter of the nineteenth century Canada was too young to be typically anything. In the end, a hybrid game emerged that established the foundation of modern Canadian football. And the Argonauts were on the front line of that process.

The history of football in Toronto dates to the first recorded game on Nov. 9, 1861, between students at the University of Toronto. They played a modified version of rugby rules with 20 players a side in which the ball

THE CONTRIBUTIONS OF THE ARGONAUT ROWING CLUB

BY GEORGE F. MCCAULEY HISTORIAN, ARGONAUT ROWING CLUB

The history of the Argonauts Football Club would be incomplete without recounting the story of the fervent band of rowers truly responsible for its founding. Their stories are one and, in fact, the football club was founded by the Argonaut Rowing Club.

Discussions about these two illustrious athletic organizations often give rise to the question: where did the name "Argonauts" originate? The answer begins in Greek mythology with the story of Jason and his crew of loyal Argonauts, who set off in the ship Argo to find the Golden Fleece. It resumes along the Thames River in England in the 1860s where a small rowing club, the Argonauts, operated briefly before being swallowed by the much larger, and still active, London Rowing Club. Finally, it wends its way to Toronto where a young lawyer named Henry O'Brien aspired to open a new rowing club.

In 1871, O'Brien became discouraged by an indifference towards competitive rowing among the majority of rowers at his club, the Toronto Rowing Club. He felt the club had become a lounging place where members talked about rowing rather than doing it, so he set about to form a new club.

During that same year, Roger and Harold Lambe, two very skilled oarsmen from the London Rowing Club, immigrated to Canada to establish a tea importing business. They learned of O'Brien's plans and showed great interest in his proposal. Along with a fourth man, Walter Nursey, they held a series of meetings at O'Brien's home, "Dromoland," on Sherbourne Street. A rough draft of bylaws was prepared and an organizational meeting was held in the Rossin House Hotel on Friday, June 21, 1872, at which the new club was duly constituted.

Roger Lambe had been a member of the London Rowing Club in the 1860s when it absorbed the cross-town Argonauts Club. He now felt it would be appropriate to resurrect the name. And so it was moved by Lambe, and seconded by Nursey, that the new Toronto club be called the Argonaut Rowing Club. The motion carried unanimously.

The next matter of business was selecting the club's colours. England was the birthplace of competitive rowing, and many rowing men in Canada at the time were English born. So, seeking a link with the old country, the Argonaut founding fathers selected the light blue of Cambridge and the dark blue of Oxford, the now famous Double Blue.

It is quite evident that these men gave much thought to the selection of the name and colours for their new club. Little could they have known at the time, however, that they had laid the foundation for a Canadian sports institution.

Three principal officers were elected at the founding meeting. O'Brien, who members nicknamed Jason, was declared president, Nursey became secretary and Lambe was elected as the first captain. In addition to being a champion oarsman, Lambe and his brother were equally proficient in the English game of rugby football. Roger Lambe decided to introduce this new game to his clubmates as an excellent means to stay fit in the fall. His proposal was quickly endorsed by his English-born clubmates, who helped the Canadian-born members quickly adapt to the new game.

What started out as simply a game to be played between members of the Argonaut Rowing Club for its fitness value soon developed into much more. Challenges began to arrive from outside rugby football clubs and many were accepted.

Because the game was received with such enthusiasm by club members, a movement began to have rugby football formally recognized as the second major sport at the Argonaut Rowing Club. At a meeting of the A.R.C. on September 17, 1874, following the conclusion of other club business, it was moved by Harold Lambe and seconded by Hugh Glazebrook "that in the opinion of this meeting it is expedient to allow gentlemen who are not members of the Argonaut Rowing Club to become members of the Argonauts Football Club on paying the subscription of one dollar, after their names have been approved by the committee of the rowing club."

The motion carried and the meeting adjourned. The Argonauts Football Club was born.

There was now a rowing club and a football club, each run by a committee appointed by and responsible to the executive of the Argonaut Rowing Club. This arrangement worked effectively for 83 years—and produced 10 Grey Cup champions—until the football club was sold to a group of Toronto businessmen in 1957.

To this day, however, the deep roots shared by the rowing and football clubs continue to prompt sportswriters when doing a story on the football Argonauts to refer with delight to the exploits of the "boatmen," the "oarsmen," and the "scullers." The connection is also evident in the Argonaut club song, *Yea Argos!* It was written and composed for the Argonaut Rowing Club by Jack Strathdee, and was first performed as a musical number by members of the rowing club in the stage presentation *The Argo Show Boat* at the Regent Theatre in April 1928. The song encourages supporters to "Fight for the old double Blue / Fight for the good old name / Fight for our football team and / Fight for our oarsmen too." From this song emerged the rallying cry: Yea Argos!

Despite several changes in ownership and management styles during the 50 years since the Argonaut Rowing Club sold the franchise, Toronto's CFL team still proudly bears the name Argonauts Football Club and still wears the traditional Double Blue. The club has remained true to its rowing origins. Henry O'Brien and Roger Lambe would be proud. May two of the greatest sports clubs in Canada continue to enjoy great success for many years to come.

Yea Argos!

THE ARGONAUT FOOTBALL CLUB SONG

Yea Argos! Yea Argos! / Fight Em, Fight Em, Fight Em Argos.
Fight for the old Double Blue. / Fight for your good old name,
Fight for your Rugby Team, And / Fight for your Oarsmen too, Yea Argos.
Yea Argos! Yea Argos!
Always pull together Argos / Out in front you'll show
You're the best Club to belong to / Oh! You Argos of Toronto
So Argos - - - Let's go.

THE ARGONAUT ROWING CLUB
Toronto 1872
PULL TOGETHER

Top Left
Argonaut Rowing Club founder Henry O'Brien.

Top Right
Roger Lambe, 1873.

could be bounced but not carried. This "local rules" game became popular on university campuses through the 1860s. When the Argonauts formed Toronto's first non-university football club in 1873 they introduced rugby rules, a 15-a-side game that more closely resembled traditional English rugby.

Canada's oldest sports rivalry was born on October 18, 1873

For many years it was generally accepted that the Argonauts' first game was played on October 11, 1873 against the University of Toronto. But that October 11 game was actually played on October 18 and the University of Toronto's participation is "the legacy of a journalistic error on the part of a Toronto newspaper," according to University of Toronto sports historian Ian Speers.

On October 18, 1873 the Argonauts played the first recorded game in their history against the Hamilton Football Club. The teams met late on a Saturday afternoon on the grounds of the University of Toronto, perhaps giving rise to the confusion about who actually played in that game. But Speers' research is definitive. Two Toronto newspapers, the *Globe* and the *Daily Mail* (which merged in 1936 to form the *Globe and Mail)* carried accounts of the game. The *Globe* stated that the Argonauts' opponent was the University of Toronto, but in comparing the *Globe* with the *Daily Mail* it is clear that the *Globe* got it wrong. The first Argonaut opponent was Hamilton, and Canada's oldest sports rivalry was born on October 18, 1873.

As for the game itself, it lasted about 90 minutes and was witnessed by a "large number" of spectators. The Argonauts' first hero was a player named Buchanan, who would suit up just one other time for Toronto. He kicked the ball through the uprights just before time elapsed to give the Double Blue its only goal, to go along with one touchdown and five rouges, against Hamilton's two rouges. (By the rules of the day, the team with the most "goals" won, and a goal was achieved by a successful kick.) The Argonauts' first captain/coach was H.T. Glazebrook. He suffered his first defeat, one goal to nil, the following week in the Argonauts' first road game, a rematch against Hamilton.

A version of the rugby rules football that the Argonauts introduced to Toronto had been growing in popularity in Montreal throughout the

Buchanan kicked the ball through the uprights just before time elapsed to give the Double Blue its only goal

Top Smirlie Lawson hurdles the line, 1909.

Above The Argonaut Rowing Club football team of 1910.

No sporting event in 1874 "caused more excitement" than Ontario against Quebec

1860s. In 1874, the most important game of the era was played when a team from McGill University went to Harvard in Cambridge, Massachusetts on May 14 for a two-game friendly series. Harvard was smitten by the McGill brand of rugby (a derivative of English rugby) and convinced other U.S. colleges to adopt the oval-ball game. The Americans soon began to modify the rules and within a few years had developed an 11-a-side game that replaced the pure brawn of traditional rugby with speed and precision ball movement. In Canada, the American developments were scorned by traditionalists but envied by others, thus setting in motion a debate that still flares today about the relative merits of the Canadian and American games.

The Argos' second season opened with a pair of goalless draws against Hamilton, followed by victories over Toronto Lacrosse and Trinity College. But the most interesting game of 1874 was an inter-provincial match between Ontario and Quebec (a quasi all-star game) that included a sizeable Argonaut contingent and represented the club's first foray outside of the province. The *Montreal Gazette*, according to Speers, reported that no sporting event in 1874 "caused more excitement" than this match, which attracted more than 1,500 spectators. Tickets cost 25-cents for men and women got in free. Each team scored one "goal" and, by the convention of the day, the game was scored a tie, despite Ontario also scoring five unconverted tries.

A second inter-provincial match in 1875 (this time won by Ontario) underlined the need to establish a unified set of rules. The issue, though, was which set of rules to adopt? The University of Toronto, for instance, had been playing a 20-a-side, rough-and-tumble game under what it called "local rules." The Argonauts, represented by their captain, Glazebrook, supported a 15-a-side game fashioned on traditional Rugby Union rules. In a meeting that included representation of all the principal clubs of Ontario and Quebec, the Argonauts' position won out, and the foundation was laid to develop a game that, as Speers notes, would become distinct from "either its English parent or American step-parent."

1899

1901

1906

1907

In the early 1880s, the traditional scrum was replaced by a line-of-scrimmage

Canadian football remained largely unstructured through the late 1870s. The Argonauts were an amateur club that played from three to five challenge matches each year against university and city teams. In 1876 and '77, their season was split almost evenly between spring and fall. But by 1878, specific references to the name "Argonauts" disappear from the records. In 1879 there is no report of the Argonauts playing a single game. Speers suggests the club may have undergone a reorganization in 1879 that left it unable to field a team, and points to an article in the *Mail* that asserts the Argonauts "gave up the ghost" after 1878. Another theory contends that the football team, still primarily comprised of Argonaut rowers, was decimated by injuries. This account is supported in a pamphlet published in 1911 by an Argonaut founder, Henry O'Brien. In his *Historical Sketch of the Argonaut Rowing Club, 1873-1911*, O'Brien says that due to football "so many of the men sustained injuries which interfered with the rowing end of the Club, that it was determined to drop it." The football club remained dormant until well into the 1890s, when the Argonaut Football Club begins to reappear in newspaper and other accounts around 1898.

Meantime, Canadian football continued to evolve. In the early 1880s, the traditional scrum was replaced by a line-of-scrimmage formation. By replacing large, plodding, brute scrums with a more open formation, in which players faced each other along a line, the ball was put into play faster, creating a more lively game predicated on speed and creativity. This change received a mixed reaction. One problem was that, at 15-a-side, the field was too crowded, so teams began to experiment with 12 players or, in some cases, even trying the U.S. style of 11 men. In the end, rules makers weren't quite ready to forego the 15-a-side game but, over the next three years, the "open formation" became standard.

Additional change followed the creation of the Ontario Rugby Football Union in 1883. Matches would henceforth be decided by a majority-points system, rather than solely by goals. The ORFU became the first North American organization to create a league structure and a playoff system to declare a true champion. That year was also notable because of the construction of a new Toronto stadium in Rosedale. At a cost of $32,000 and with a seating capacity of 2,000, the Rosedale field would be a primary site for football in Toronto until Varsity Stadium was renovated in 1911.

These developments, however, did not quiet the clamour to make the Canadian game more closely conform with the evolving U.S. style of play. In 1884, Harvard played an exhibition in Ottawa and, for half the game, American 11-a-side college rules were employed, which permitted, among other things, a quarterback to pick up the ball in a scrum and snap it into play. Some ORFU members proposed the adoption of the snap back and other U.S. innovations, but they were defeated.

Still, throughout the 1880s and 1890s, as the concept of inter-city, league and national championship play evolved, the game was changing. In 1890, Toronto's Edward Bayly returned from a fact-finding mission to the annual Yale-Princeton match to recommend that the ORFU embrace some "minor" modifications, including the adoption of 11-a-side play (from 15) and reduction in the size of the playing field. Bayly's recommendations were rejected but the desire remained strong among many to mimic American rules. Battle lines were drawn: the modernizers were pitted against the traditionalists. Their wrangling stretched out over the ensuing decades and brought an outcome neither might have predicted. They built a uniquely Canadian game.

INTER-PROVINCIAL
RUGBY
UNION

Official Program
SEASON 1907

ATHLETIC FIELD
TORONTO

Right
The Argonauts, circa 1908-09.

The Argonauts, meanwhile, reactivated their football club sometime in the mid-1890s and by 1898 had rejoined the ORFU. By 1900 they had reclaimed their place among the nation's top clubs, led by Joe Wright, one of the top all-round athletes in the country; Percy (Pug) Hardisty, who, against Hamilton in 1900, rushed for 180 yards on 12 carries; centre-half C.W. Darling, Laurie Boyd and Pud Kent. But the Argos were back on the sidelines in 1903 following a dispute about professionalism.

Football was a strictly amateur pastime at the turn of the century. Rules

The Rosedale field cost $32,000 and had a seating capacity of 2,000

forbade players to accept payment for playing any sport, not just football. But it was not uncommon for hockey or baseball teams to slip a little something to their top players, and nor was it uncommon for fine athletes to play multiple sports. Many football clubs, including the Argonauts, were willing to look the other way so as not to lose top athletes to the "professional" leagues. The dispute came to a head in 1903 and the Argonauts withdrew from the ORFU in protest.

They returned in 1904 but the amateur-versus-professional debate continued to simmer and was a factor when Toronto, along with Hamilton, Ottawa and Montreal, broke away from the ORFU in 1907 to form the new Interprovincial Rugby Football Union. These were the four most powerful non-collegiate teams in the country and thus the IRFU became known the Big Four. The first star of the new IRFU was an

Argonaut, a fleet back named Peter Flett, who ran for 195 yards in a game against Hamilton and led the league in scoring with 29 points.

The Big Four represented the most powerful club teams in the land but they were no stronger than top collegiate squads from such schools as the University of Toronto, Queen's and McGill. So when the Governor-General of Canada, Earl Grey, donated a silver trophy in 1909 to be contested among the top amateur teams in the country, it was no surprise that the U of T won the Grey Cup the first three years. Their third championship, in 1911, spoiled the Grey Cup debut of the Argonauts.

Top The 1911 Argos.

Below Varsity Stadium, 1911.

Far left Mike Rodden, coach and player, 1919-20.

Left Chaucer Elliott, coach, 1906 & 1910.

Lower left William Foulds, coach and player, 1911.

Opposite page Joe A. Wright, 1898-1902.

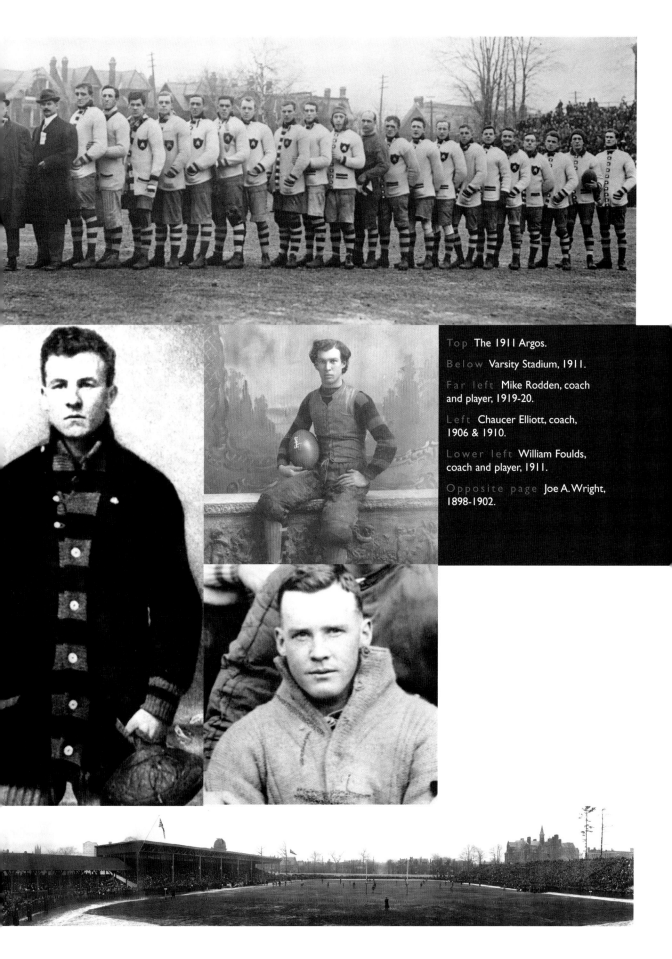

The Argonauts had advanced to their first Grey Cup that year largely on the kicking of Ross Binkley and running of Smirle Lawson, the original "Big Train." Binkley's league-leading 34 points included a then-remarkable 52-yard field goal. Lawson was a fierce backfielder who starred for the U of T's Grey Cup champions in 1909 and 1910 before moving to the Argonauts, becoming the team captain and leading them into three Grey Cup finals in four years.

Everett Smith and Glad Murphy combined to complete a 130-yard, two-man punt return

A Canadian record crowd of 13,687 packed the newly opened Varsity Stadium for the 1911 battle of Toronto gridiron titans. But a snowstorm on the eve of the Grey Cup game caused treacherous footing and a fumble-laden contest. The conditions exacted a particularly high toll on the Argos when fumbles by Billy Mallett and Binkley near the Argos' goal line led to a pair of opposition tries, and all the scoring they'd need in a 14-7 win.

The Argonauts guaranteed that 1912 would be memorable even before they returned to the Grey Cup final. A regular-season game against Ottawa turned into a punting contest that remains unique in football history. Combined, the two teams punted 89 times for 1,760 yards in a 23-11 Toronto victory. After placing first with a 5-1 record, the Argos defeated their cross-town nemesis, U of T, in a semi-final and advanced to the Grey Cup against the Hamilton Alerts at the Hamilton Cricket Grounds. The Argos were heavy favourites but lost 11-4.

Following a sub-par 1913 season, the Argos got all the bounces in 1914 en route to finally winning their first Grey Cup. Led by their star runner and kicker Jack O'Connor, who scored a league-record 44 points, the Argos were 5-1 on the season and scored a league record 145 points. But it was a playoff punt return against Hamilton that made the most indelible mark on the record book. Starting twenty yards deep in the Argo end zone, Everett Smith ran the ball to the Argos 30-yard line and, as he was being tackled, lateralled to Glad Murphy, who went 80 yards to complete a 130-yard, two-man punt return.

Advancing to their third Grey Cup final in four years, the Argonauts again faced the U of T. But in a reversal of their 1911 meeting, the U of T fumbled away victory in 1914 as Toronto's Murphy and Freddie Mills each returned first-half fumbles for touchdowns. The Argos won 14-2 to claim their first Grey Cup trophy.

Following a three-year suspension of play during World War I, the Argonauts returned with a strong team led by Dunc Monroe and Harry Batstone and, in 1920, again faced the U of T in the Grey Cup. It was the Argonauts' fourth appearance in eight Grey Cups and the third time they'd faced the U of T. The rubber match was no contest. On a drizzly afternoon at Varsity Stadium, a crowd of 10,000 saw U of T shut down the vaunted Argonauts offence to win 16-3.

With that game, Canadian football turned a significant page in its history. The era when students could compete with men was over. The U of T would not win another Grey Cup. Arrival of the 1921 season brought new rules to open up the game and a new mandate to open up the national championship to powerhouse western teams like the Edmonton Eskimos and Winnipeg Bombers. It also brought a new influx of stars, first among them a bruising backfielder named Lionel Conacher.

~ Jim O'Leary

Above The first Argonaut Grey Cup champions, 1914.

Argos on the move, 1912.

SECTION 3

3

1921–1952

All Aboard

When people speak of the Roaring Twenties, they aren't talking about Canadian football—but they could be.

That is when the game firmly took root in the hearts and minds of football fans across the country. It was a time when star players blossomed, franchises matured, rules evolved, the east-west Grey Cup was born and the modern game emerged. Continuously beating at the heart of this awakening was Canada's oldest franchise, the Toronto Argonauts.

From 1921 to 1952, the Argos went to nine Grey Cup games, and won every one of them. They were Canada's dominant franchise and had a knack for attracting the game's biggest stars: Harry Batstone, Cap Fear, Dunc Monroe, Joe Breen in the '20s; Teddy Morris, Bob Isbister, the Stukus brothers—Annis, Bill and Frank—Ab Box, Wes Cutler, Lew Hayman, and Red Storey in the '30s; the matchless Gold Dust Twins, Joe Krol and Royal Copeland, Frank Morris, and Bill Zock in the '40s; Al Dekdebrun, Nobby Wirkowski and Ulysses Curtis in the early '50s. At one time or another, each of those men ruled the field, but none quite so thoroughly as the incomparable Lionel Conacher.

Conacher arrived at his first Argos training camp in 1921 from a Toronto working-class neighbourhood as a strapping 6-foot-1, 200-pound, 20-year-old already established as one of Toronto's finest all-round athletes. A champion in boxing, wrestling and lacrosse, he turned down pro offers from the National Hockey League Toronto St. Pats and the American League Detroit Tigers to play for the then amateur Argonauts.

Conacher's rookie season coincided with a watershed year for

Left
Harry Batstone, 1919-21.

Previous page
The wholesome Argos of 1946, left to right, Art Skidmore, Tom Glenn, Les Ascott, Fred Doty and Bruce Richardson.

A YANKEE THRASHING

THIRD CORPS TEAM CRUSHES ARGONAUTS

Three Touchdowns in First Ten Minutes Decide Game at Yankee Stadium.

FINAL SCORE IS 55 TO 7

Canadians' Fumbling on Lateral Passes Proves Disastrous—Noyes and Dodd Shine.

Yankee Stadium, opened in 1923, is universally known as the House That Ruth Built in tribute to baseball legend Babe Ruth. But for the Toronto Argonauts, taking on the Third Army Corps in a November 4th afternoon exhibition game that inaugural year, Yankee Stadium was a House of Horrors.

Facing a team comprised primarily of West Point graduates, the Argos, led by Lionel Conacher, were in over their heads in many ways (wearing caps to their opponents' helmets, for one), and were spanked, 55-7. The Americans scored in the first three minutes and had three touchdowns by the 10-minute mark.

"The Canadians were at a loss to solve the crisscross, off tackle, fake pass and end run plays," explained *The New York Times* the following day.

The only Argos score came in the second quarter, "the result of some baffling lateral passing." In just five plays, the Toronto squad marched from their own five-yard line to the Army 25-yard line. Dunc Monroe, the left halfback, broke through on a fake pass and made the end zone untouched.

Top left Dunc Monroe (1919-20 & 1923) prepares to punt as the Argos face the Third Army Corps at Yankee Stadium, 1923.

Top, above and right The incomparable Lionel "Big Train" Conacher, an Argo for two seasons, 1921-22.

Below 1921 Grey Cup Champions, after beating the Edmonton Eskimos 23-0 at Varsity Stadium.

Canadian football. After decades of debate, American-style rule changes saw on-field lineups reduced from 14 players to 12, the introduction of the snap back into the hands of the quarterback from between the legs of the centre, and the establishment of a three-yard blocking zone (rather than the old one yard) along the line of scrimmage. The intent was to generate more offence. The effect was to stoke perhaps the greatest team in Argo history, led by Conacher, their Big Train.

The 1921 Argonauts went 6-0 in the regular season, setting a Canadian football record of 167 points, including romps of 45-2 and 42-0 over Montreal. (Add in the playoffs and Grey Cup and the Argos outscored opponents 226-55.) Conacher alone had 49.7% of the team's offence, scoring 85 points and 14 touchdowns, both records. In his first game he scored 23 of the Argos' 27 points and, leaving the field, reportedly said he had "as much fun as a pickerel in a minnow pond."

The game had never seen a backfield like that of the 1921 Argonauts. They boasted the trio of Conacher, Harry Batstone and Cap Fear, all of whom reside today in the Canadian Football Hall of Fame. Quarterback Shrimp Cochrane would ignite the running game by getting the ball to his running backs. The favourite play was a pitch to Batstone, the team captain, who would either plough through the line himself or pitch to Conacher. In full flight, his powerful legs churning like pistons, Conacher was almost unstoppable. He never saw the merit in feigning or deking. His approach was simple. Lock onto a straight track and dare anyone to derail him. Few could.

"He had size, speed, fierce determination and a perfect frame for

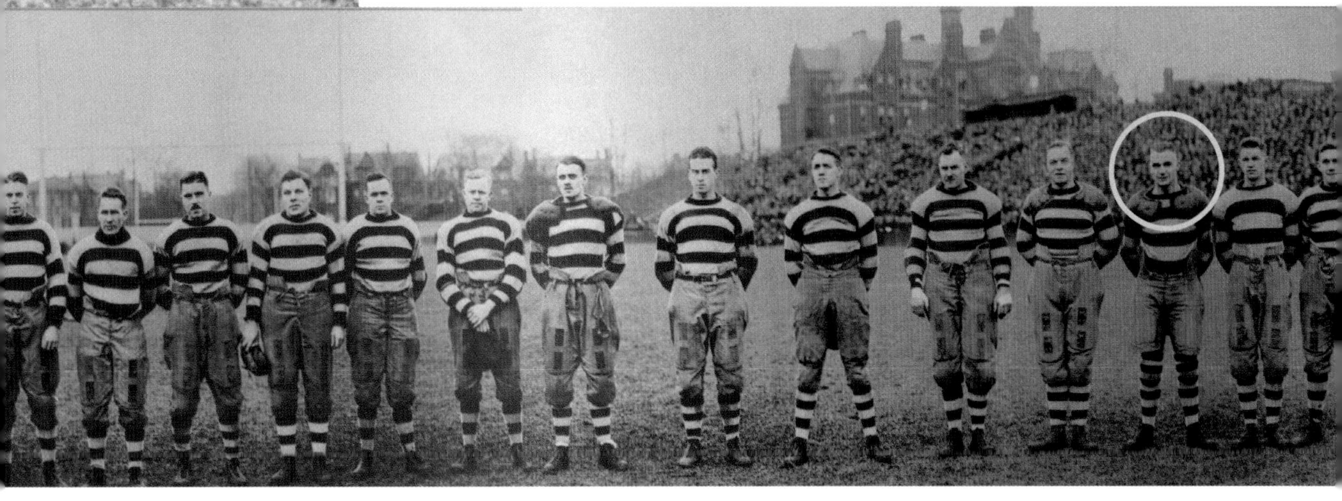

team sports," his brother Charlie once said. "He had perfectly set legs with Clydesdale thighs."

He had perfectly set legs with Clydesdale thighs

In the 1921 playoffs, the Argos defeated the University of Toronto 20-12 and Parkdale 16-8 to push their season record to 8-0 and advance to the Grey Cup. It was the first ever East-West final, with the Edmonton Eskimos advancing to Varsity Stadium. The day belonged to Conacher. Playing in what would be his only Grey Cup game, Conacher scored 17 points (two five-point touchdowns, one field goal and four singles) in a 23-0 Toronto victory. He played the full 60 minutes and, immediately after the game, grabbed his skates and rushed off to play defence for a local club in the Senior Ontario Hockey Association.

Conacher would play only two years for the Argos before signing a lucrative NHL contract and embarking on a Hall of Fame hockey career. His best individual football season was 1922 when he ran for 950 yards in a six-game schedule (an average of 158 yards per game) and then added 232 yards on 35 carries in a 12-11 semi-final loss to Queen's. In that game, Conacher broke free with less than a minute to play with only one player between him and the game-winning touchdown. That player was Harry Batstone, Conacher's 1921 running mate who had defected to Queen's in 1922. Few players could stop Conacher in the open field but Batstone, a tremendous all-round athlete in his own right, made a diving tackle to end the Argos' season.

By the end of the 1920s there was a growing clamour for rule changes to further open up the game. In particular, the modernizers yearned for the American-style forward pass and downfield blocking, both of which were finally adopted in 1931. The first Argo forward pass—Teddy Morris to Bill Darling—was completed on October 10 of that year against Hamilton. But for the most part the Argos regarded the forward pass as a gimmick. Their first touchdown pass—Andy Mullan to Jack Taylor—wasn't completed until 1933, and even then passing played a minor role as the Argos, under coach Lew Hayman, won their third Grey Cup. Their 1933 title came the old fashioned way, courtesy of the power running and punting of Ab Box, the best kicker of his era. He led the Argos to a 4-3

Left
A. H. "Cap" Fear, 1919-25.

Below
Harry Hutchingham of Ottawa eludes the Argo posse, 1924.

Grey Cup win over the Sarnia Imperials in icy conditions.

The Argos fielded competitive teams throughout the 1930s and peaked in 1937 and '38 with the first back-to-back Grey Cup championships in club history. The anchors of those teams were backfielders Teddy Morris and Art West, backed by the Stukus boys, Bill, Annis and Frank. Morris was a hard-as-nails running back/linebacker who would win six Grey Cups as an Argo, three as a player and three more as a coach. West made three interceptions in his 1936 Argos debut, and then became an offensive star, leading the league in touchdowns in '37 and '38. Between them, the Stukus boys—or the Stukii, as they called themselves—played just about every position on the field during their years together with the Argos. One year, Annis made starts at seven different positions. Their best year was 1938, when they not only made history by becoming the Grey Cup's first three-brother act, but they did mama Stukus proud during a game in Montreal by combining for four touchdowns, one each by Annis and Frank, and two by Bill.

Hayman's Argos encountered no serious opposition in 1937, going 5-1 in the regular season before defeating Ottawa and Sarnia in the playoffs to advance to the Grey Cup championship. Held on a cold, December 11 afternoon, it was a fumble-prone affair in which Toronto defeated Winnipeg 4-3, the difference being a single by Bob Isbister. The same teams met again in 1938 in a game that saw an Argo benchwarmer spark one of the most improbable finishes in club history.

Red Storey was a second-string running back on that powerful 1938 team. In the Grey Cup, his uniform was washday clean when he entered the game to start the fourth quarter. The Argos trailed 7-6 and had given no hint of being able to crack a granite-tough Winnipeg defence. Then Storey took over. He received a lateral from quarterback Bill Stukus and went 28 yards for a touchdown. Minutes later, Storey intercepted a Winnipeg pass and returned the ball to within four yards of the goalline, from where he plunged over for his second touchdown. Next, Isbister intercepted a pass on the Argo five-yard line and, being tackled, flipped the ball to Storey, who went 100 yards to the Winnipeg five, scoring his

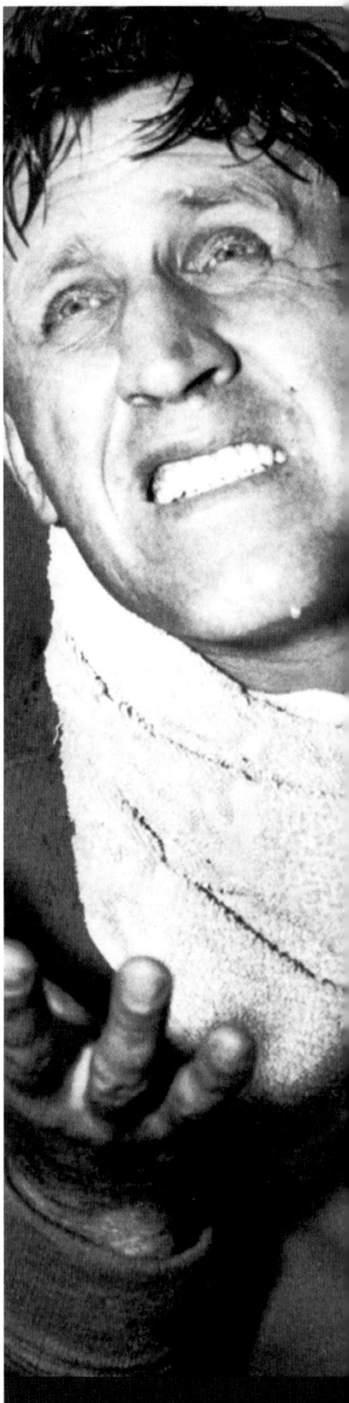

Above
Annis Stukus.

Above right
Joe Breen rambles upfield, 1925.

Far right
Ted Reeve (left) and an unknown player for Balmy Beach, 1923.

Right Ab Box, 1932-34.

NOTICE

MUDDYING IT UP AGAINST THE REGINA ROUGHRIDERS, 1933

BATTLING THE OTTAWA ROUGH RIDERS THE SAME SEASON, 1933

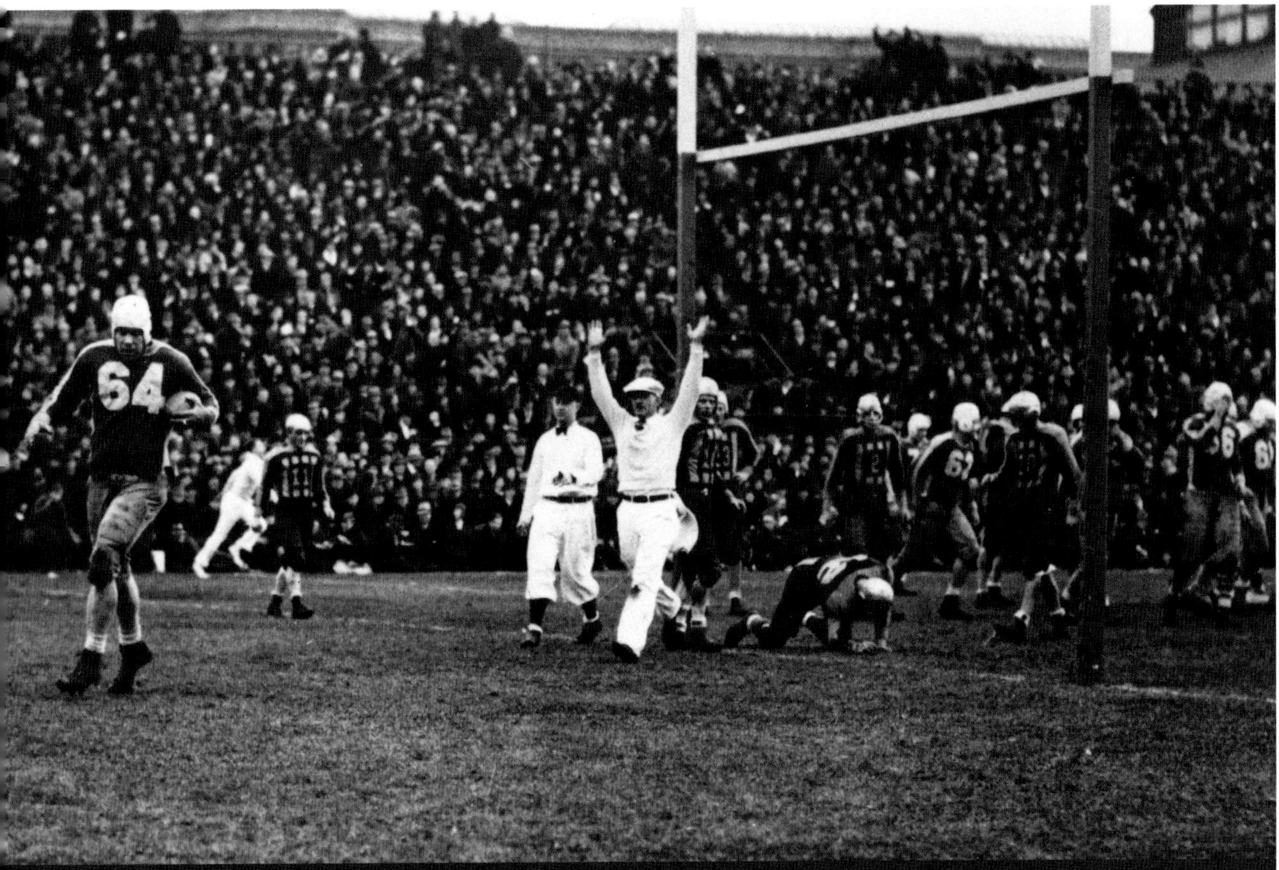

ONE OF RED STOREY'S THREE TOUCHDOWN ROMPS, GREY CUP, 1938

third touchdown on the next play. Storey made another long run to set up a fourth Argo touchdown. The final: 30-7, with Storey scoring 15 fourth-quarter points.

League play was suspended during World War II and when it resumed the Argos assembled their first true dynasty, becoming the first team to win three consecutive Grey Cups (1945, '46, '47) and five championships in eight years. There was certainly no mystery to the Argos post-war success. They flat-footed teams with the Gold Dust Twins, Joe (King) Krol and Royal Copeland. Krol and Copeland, or Copeland and Krol, were interchangeable stars in the Argos' backfield. Each could run, pass and catch the ball. When teams focused on one, the other broke free. "Whether it was Krol passing to Copeland or Copeland passing to Krol, they were the devil to defend," wrote Jim Coleman. The post-game summaries were just as likely to record touchdown passes from Krol to Copeland as Copeland to Krol.

The pair had warmed up for the 1945 Grey Cup by a season-ending victory in which Copeland caught 10 passes for 147 yards, including four touchdown throws from Krol. Against Winnipeg in the Grey Cup game, a 35-0 Argos victory, Krol threw two touchdown passes (worth five points each at the time) and returned an interception for a touchdown; Copeland contributed a 15-yard touchdown run.

It was much the same the following year. Again Toronto met Winnipeg in the Grey Cup and, again, Krol and Copeland dominated. The scoring opened with a Krol to Copeland touchdown pass and, following a Krol interception, the two reversed roles, with Copeland throwing a touchdown strike to Krol. Krol would throw two more touchdown passes (to Rod Smylie and Boris Tipoff), but perhaps the game's most memorable play was a perfectly executed onside punt from the foot of Krol to the hands of—you guessed it—Copeland at Winnipeg's one-yard line, setting up a touchdown plunge by Byron Karrys. Final score: 28-6.

By 1947 Winnipeg must have been wondering if it was really worth making the trip to Toronto to face Krol and Copeland in another Grey Cup. This time, though, the Bombers made a game of it. Winnipeg led 9-1 at halftime. Then Krol hit Copeland with a 38-yard touchdown pass to make it 9-7. A pair of Argos' singles made it 9-9 with two minutes left in the game. With seconds remaining, the Bombers gambled—and were stopped—on third and one from their own 25-yard line, allowing Krol to kick a game-winning single as the game ended.

"Joe did EVERYTHING," said teammate Charlie Camilleri. "He ran, passed, punted, kicked field goals, played defence. Only Jackie Parker came close to his versatility."

Throughout the 1940s, Argos coach Teddy Morris refused to follow the league trend to fill key positions with U.S. players. So his championship teams were all-Canadian. But when the Argos slipped to third place in 1948 and '49, and the league increased the import quota from five to seven Americans for the 1950 season, ownership replaced Morris with American Frank Clair. Not only did he sprinkle the roster with imports, including quarterback Al Dekdebrun, but Clair also

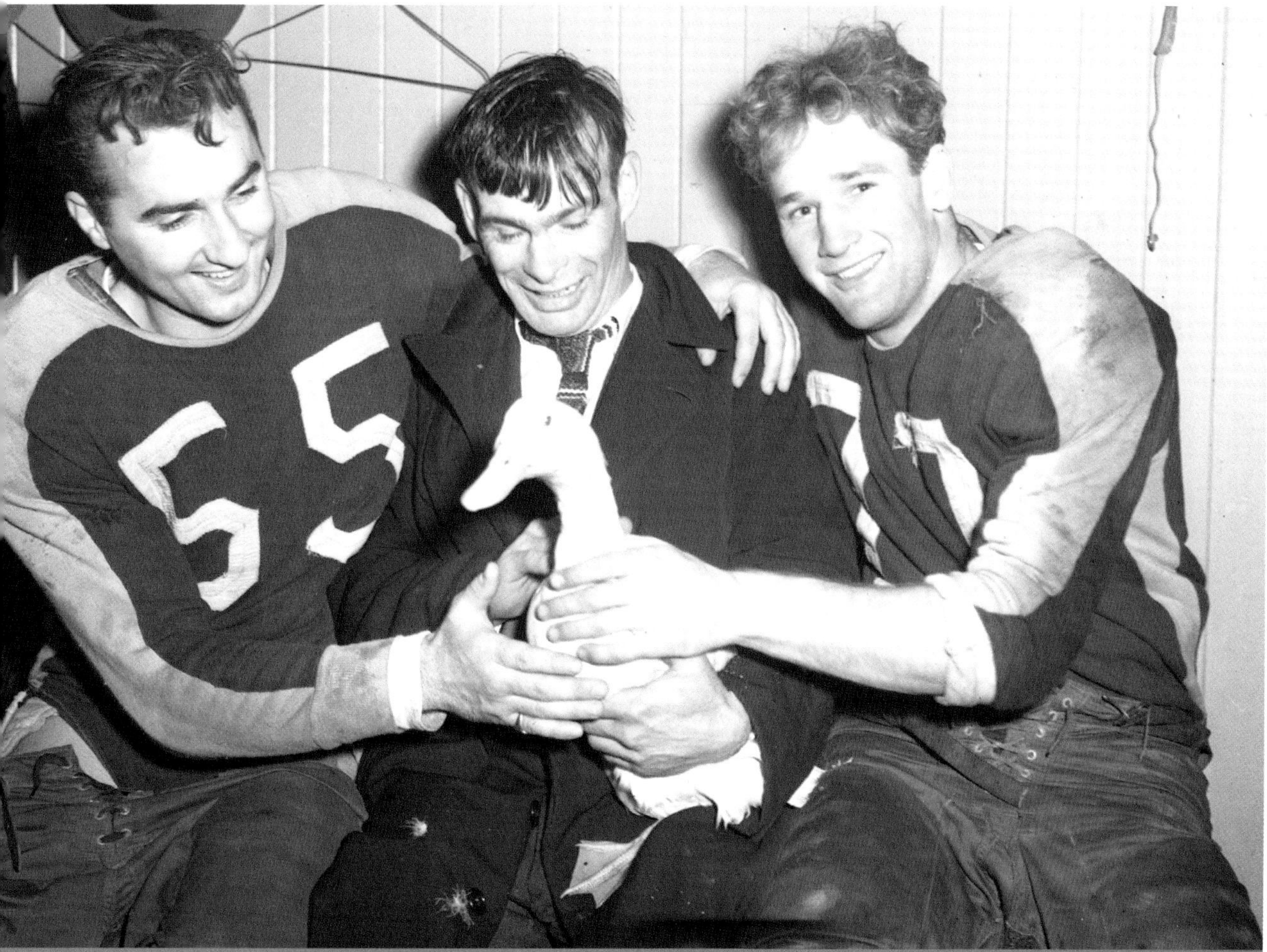

JOE KROL, TEDDY MORRIS AND ROYAL COPELAND FEELING DUCKY, LATE 1940s

ARGO MEMORY

ULYSSES CURTIS

Although I was a running back, coach Frank Clair would play me on defence... most players played on both sides of the ball in those days.

I remember a game at the end of the 1951 season at Varsity Stadium against Ottawa. It was very close. Late in the game I intercepted a pass by Ottawa's quarterback Tom O'Malley that would ultimately lead to a new rule.

I was heading down the field when Ottawa's Peter Karpuk came off their bench and took a shot at me! There was nothing in the books to deal with the situation, and the officials were huddled for the longest time trying to figure it out.

Finally, they awarded us the ball half the distance to the goal line, and Ottawa had to play one man short for two minutes like they do in hockey. Our quarterback, Nobby Wirkowski, handed off to Teddy Toogood on the next play and we took the lead on the way to a 23-18 win.

Right Ulysses Curtis, 1950-54.

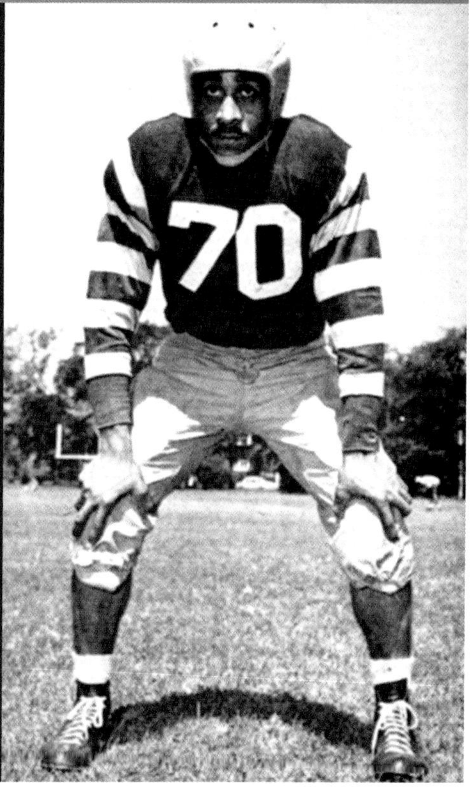

FAN MEMORY

THE ARGOS — CHOICE OF THE DENTISTS

Growing up in Manitoba, Bert J. Levin was a Blue Bombers fan. But having come to study at the University of Toronto in 1941 to become a dentist, he switched allegiances. After his discharge from the Canadian military in 1947, he became an Argonauts season ticket holder—which he still is today. Bert is as passionate as ever. "My family knows that I'm not touchable during any game," he says. "I love the game and am a great believer in Canadian football."

From the late '40s into the '50s, Bert was the ringleader of a group of fans at Varsity Stadium who knew more than a little about pain.

"In a few years, I increased my subscription to about 20-odd guys, that were all dentists," he said. "We all went to the games, and sat in a great, big square section there, two or three rows, pretty compact. Everybody had their tickets. We all went with our wives."

ARGO MEMORY

CHARLIE CAMILLERI

I have several vivid memories.

I remember a game in Ottawa. It was freezing cold, somewhere between rain and snow. We were dipping our feet in buckets of water to thaw them out.

Another time we were playing Balmy Beach in an ORFU playoff game. I cracked a Balmy Beach ball carrier pretty good—but it rang my bell! I was all woozy, and my knees were giving out. They were asking me the old "how many fingers..."

My career came to a close in 1947 after my teammate Billy Briggs broke my pelvis in practice. You weren't supposed to hit a quarterback! That put me out for most of the season. I came back for one game after that and packed it in.

Left Charlie Camilleri, 1946-48, and Billy Briggs, 1945 & 1947-49.

Below The Mud Bowl.

FAN MEMORY

BY NORMAN RUBINOFF

On a cold and rainy day in November of 1950, I took the streetcar from my house at Queen and Roncesvalles to Varsity Stadium where my hometown Argos were facing the Winnipeg Blue Bombers in the 1950 Grey Cup game. I went up into the rain-soaked benches in the bleachers to watch the two teams battle for the ultimate prize.

I remember thinking to myself at the time that this was one of the poorest games I had ever witnessed. The game was filled with errors, namely fumbles as players from both teams slipped and slid in the mud-covered field. By the time the fourth quarter arrived, it was difficult to see some of the players' jerseys as both teams were now wearing uniforms soaked in mud.

The game ended with the home team prevailing 13-0 and despite all the errors and mishaps, I now think back and am proud that I was part of history. Today, the 1950 Grey Cup game in Toronto is simply known as the "Mud Bowl."

brought talented black players to Toronto, led by a mesmerizing running back named Ulysses (Crazy Legs) Curtis. Krol was relegated to the role of punter and Copeland, the first player to score a touchdown in three consecutive Grey Cup games, was traded to Calgary.

The payoff was immediate. After placing second with a 6-5-1 record, and scoring a club record 209 points (the old record of 167 points had stood since the six-game season of 1921), the Argos defeated Hamilton and Balmy Beach in the playoffs to return to the Grey Cup. Once again their opponent was Winnipeg, led by Indian Jack Jacobs and a vaunted aerial attack. Anticipation ran high for a classic showdown, and the game was indeed memorable—but for all the wrong reasons. Toronto was hit by a snowstorm during Grey Cup week. Work crews decided to plough the snow from the Varsity Stadium field and only succeeded in ripping up the turf. The arrival of mild temperatures turned the field into a bog.

Today, that game—the Mud Bowl—is recalled with a smile. But no one was laughing in 1950, with the possible exception of Teddy Morris. The quagmire eliminated the precision passing and slick running that the American imports were supposed to have brought to Canadian football. One Winnipeg player, Buddy Tinsley, landed face down in the muck and, apparently unconscious, lay there until the referee flipped him over before Tinsley drowned.

The field was a mess and the game was a shambles. Winnipeg's hot-shot quarterback, Jacobs, could barely hold onto the ball, fumbling twice and throwing an interception before being replaced. He completed just two passes in 11 attempts for 21 yards. Dekdebrun threw just three passes and instead kept handing off to his puddle-jumping backfield. Unlike Jacobs, Dekdebrun's grip on the ball was firm, raising some eyebrows.

"Al taped thumbtacks onto his fingertips so he could hold the ball," remembered teammate Nick Volpe. "The officials got suspicious and they checked Al's hands and they saw what he had done. They made him remove the thumbtacks in the second half so we were on a par with them."

Dekdebrun scored the game's lone touchdown and Volpe added a pair of field goals. But many observers said the difference, other than

THE INFAMOUS MUD BOWL AT VARSITY STADIUM, 1950

ARGO MEMORY

NICK VOLPE

I'll never forget the Mud Bowl of 1950. There had been six inches of snow the night before the Grey Cup and then it got mild, leaving the field covered in slushy snow.

Attempts to shovel it off proved hopeless. Small snowplows were brought in, which turned up the turf something awful. We were left with a field of mud.

I was the field-goal kicker and, although it was difficult to get the ball off the ground, I did manage to kick two field goals in two attempts. I missed a convert, though, but with the mud you didn't know which way the ball was going.

The highlight for me was making a tackle on Lee McPhail. Winnipeg was scrimmaging around midfield and McPhail broke through the line and was going for a touchdown. I was playing on the other side of the field as a safety, but managed to get close enough to dive at him and bring him down at the 10-yard line with a flying tackle. They didn't score and we won 13-0.

Coach Frank Clair gave me the game ball. I still have that ball today.

Right Nick Volpe, 1949-52.

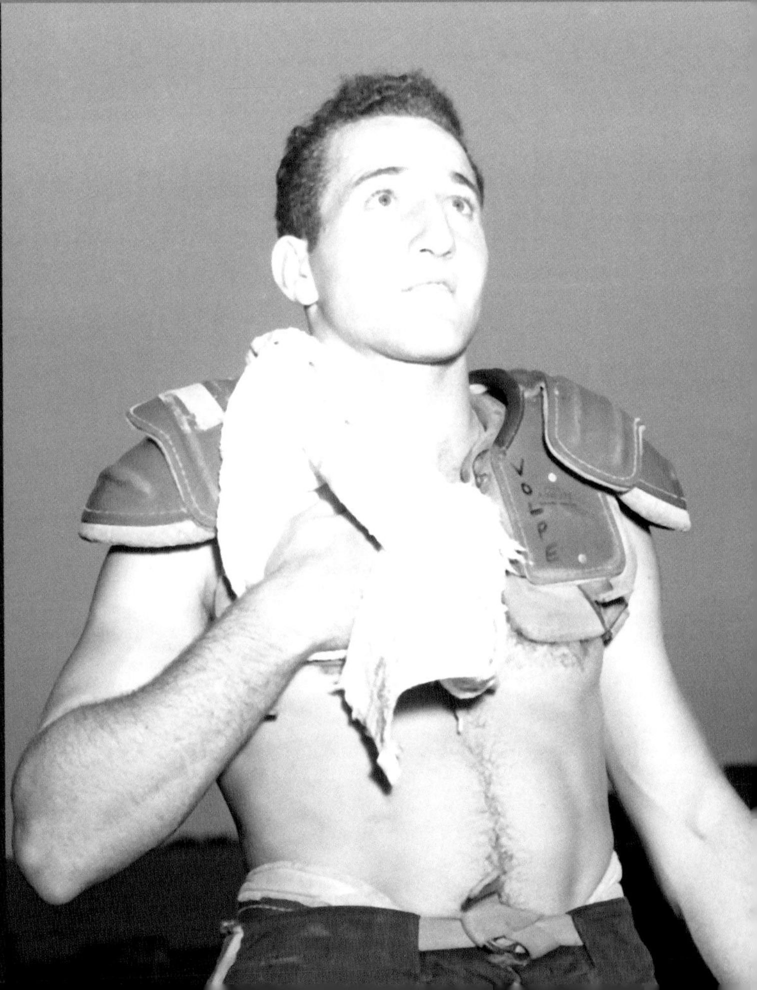

thumbtacks, was an Argo punting game that had a sprinkle of Gold Dust. Jacobs had as much trouble kicking the water-logged ball as throwing it and was consistently out-booted by the King himself, Joe Krol.

With their 13-0 Mud Bowl win, the Argos had won four of the six Grey Cups played since the end of the war and seemed poised to keep racking up the championships. Coach Frank Clair had re-tooled a well-oiled machine led by a rifle-armed quarterback named Nobby Wirkowski and the will-o-wisp running back, Crazy Legs Curtis. The Argos returned to the title game in 1952 after a 7-4-1 season in which Curtis set records for rushing (985 yards, averaging 7.8 yards per carry) and touchdowns (16). It was not so much a case of happy days being here again but being here still. In Toronto, Grey Cup appearances were regarded not so much as signs of success but confirmations of destiny.

For the most part, the 1952 Grey Cup belonged to the two defences. The Edmonton Eskimos shut down Curtis and the Argos did likewise to Edmonton's vaunted attackers Johnnie Bright and Normie Kwong. Argos led 15-11 late in the fourth quarter but the momentum seemed to be going in favour of the Eskimos. Then an Argo interception set up a game-clinching touchdown. Wirkowski spotted Zeke O'Connor totally alone deep in Edmonton territory after a breakdown in the Eskimos coverage. The pass was on the mark and the Argos won 21-11.

Toronto was now 10-0 in Grey Cup appearances since 1921 and, as 27,291 people filed out of Varsity Stadium, nothing seemed particularly distinctive about that 1952 game. It would take many years for the game's significance to sink in. It was only after the 1950s turned into the '60s and rolled into the '70s, and the Argos failed to return to the Grey Cup, that the exploits of Wirkowski and O'Connor became special.

O'Connor's touchdown marked the end of an era, though no one knew it at the time.

~ Jim O'Leary

THE GREAT ARGONAUT ROWING CLUB FIRE

BY H. M. "BO" WESTLAKE

In the very early morning hours of Tuesday, March 25, 1947, the Argonaut Rowing Club was totally destroyed by fire. Fuelled to fierce intensity by dozens of highly varnished, Spanish cedar racing shells in the lower level boathouse, the fire consumed everything—every shell, every oar, every piece of rowing equipment except for a few metal rowing machines.

The upper level, with its magnificent lounge and beautiful ballroom that boasted what was considered the best dance floor in Toronto, was also lost. The trophy lounge housed almost all the club's magnificent collection of championship shields, banners and spectacular trophies won during the club's storied 75-year history—many of the trophies really outstanding examples of the silversmith's art. They were in huge glass-fronted cabinets and, with a pathetically few exceptions, were all lost—melted to shapeless blobs of silver by heat so intense that it actually melted the glass in the cabinets.

But one trophy that miraculously survived was the Grey Cup, which had been won in 1946 (and in fact in 1945 and 1947) by the great Argonaut teams of that era. Since the football team was then owned by the rowing club and was run by the club's football committee, the Grey Cup was kept in the club's trophy lounge.

The story of the fire filled the pages of Toronto newspapers and, of course, told of the saving of the Grey Cup. An imaginative reporter, making full use of poetic licence, recounted how a fireman with a long pole reached into the raging flames and hooked the Cup into the arms of Joe Wright, Jr., one of the club's greatest rowing and football heroes.

It added a great touch of drama to what was of itself already a very dramatic event—but unfortunately, his version of the Grey Cup's salvation was completely untrue.

I know that for a fact because the Grey Cup was actually recovered from the ruins by Jim "The Indian" Millar and myself some hours *after* the fire was out and all the firemen gone.

I lived two or three blocks from the club and first heard of the disaster on the 8 a.m. news that morning. I rushed down to the lake only to find the devastation was worse than I could possibly have imagined.

There was nothing left but a huge pile of twisted, blackened rubble and ashes down on the concrete floor of the boathouse against the huge concrete retaining wall that had formed the back wall of the boathouse. A few sections of the back wall of the second level still stood precariously on the top of the retaining wall and the stairs that ran down the outside of the west wall from the top of the hill to the dock, and from which the entrance into the clubrooms had opened were still there.

Standing on the dock with Millar, we noticed a round black object that seemed to be hanging below a window frame. We went up the stairs and across the top of the retaining wall to discover a huge brass shield bearing the club's galleon crest that had always hung on the back wall of the trophy lounge. It was completely blackened and badly charred. With the Indian holding my belt and the shell of the wall shaking, I leaned through the window frame and pulled it back out. As we started back down the stairs we noticed a few blackened cups and trophies, so the Indian, who was a lot lighter than me (and a lot crazier), gingerly edged out onto the bit of the floor that remained and passed them back to me.

One of them was the storied Grey Cup—smoke blackened, slightly misshapen, its wooden base reduced to charcoal, but unmistakable. We took it and a couple of ornate old rowing trophies that also survived directly across Lakeshore Blvd. to the home of Joe Wright, Jr. He was a governor of the Canadian Rugby Union (as the CFL was then known) and he arranged to have the Grey Cup restored in time to be presented to the 1947 Canadian champions Argos.

And that is how the Grey Cup was really recovered from the razed Argonaut Rowing Club almost sixty years ago. The story lacks the dramatic impact of the newspaper account of the day but it does have one distinct advantage—it's true!

Right Joe Wright Jr. (1923-33 & 1936) with the recovered Grey Cup, 1947.

Images
1921-1952

Lift your glasses, catch those passes

Above Bill Darling, 1929-31.

Left Wes Cutler, 1933-38.

Above right
Teddy Morris, 1931-39.

Far right
Frank Turville, 1928-31.

SONG NO. 2, 1938 PROGRAM

CHEER, CHEER FOR OLD ARGONAUTS

Cheer, cheer for old Argonauts,
Mix up the cocktails, pour in the Scotch,
Send somebody out for gin,
Don't let a sober person in.
We never faulter, we never fail,
We sober up on wood alcohol.
Lift your glasses, catch those passes,
Onward to victory.

Cheer, cheer for old Argonauts,
Mix up the milk shakes, pour in the malt.
Send somebody out for "cokes,"
Don't let them in, if they tell dirty jokes,
We never smoke and we never swear,
We always wear our pink underwear
(so help us)
Lift your glasses, catch those passes,
Onward to victory.

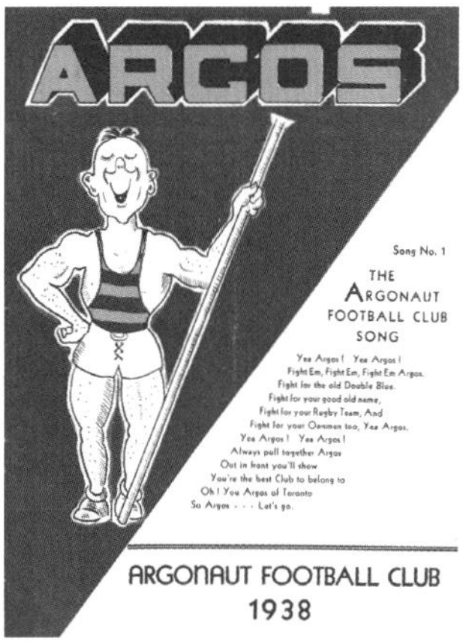

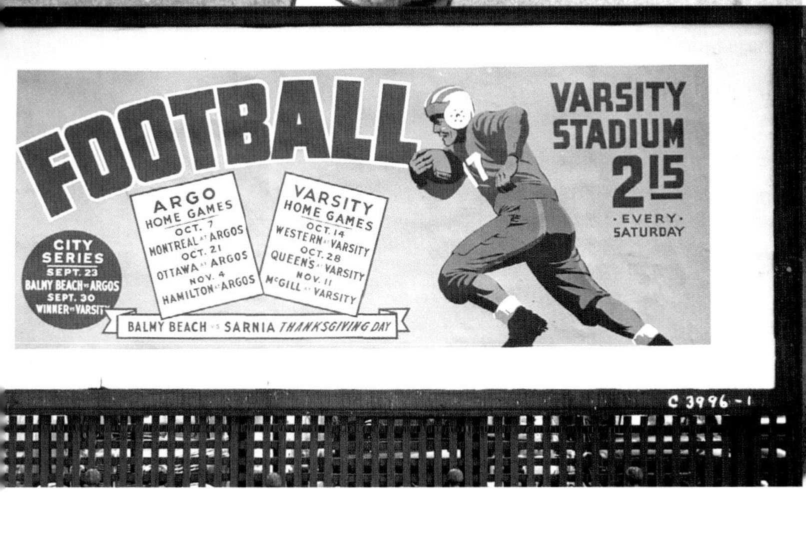

Top left Art "Whipper" West and friend, late 1930s.

Top right The famed Stukii family—Bill (1936-41 & 1947), Annis (1935-41) and Frank (1938-39 & 1941).

Bottom The triple threat that was Buster "Red" Storey, hero of the 1938 Grey Cup and an Argo from 1936 to 1941.

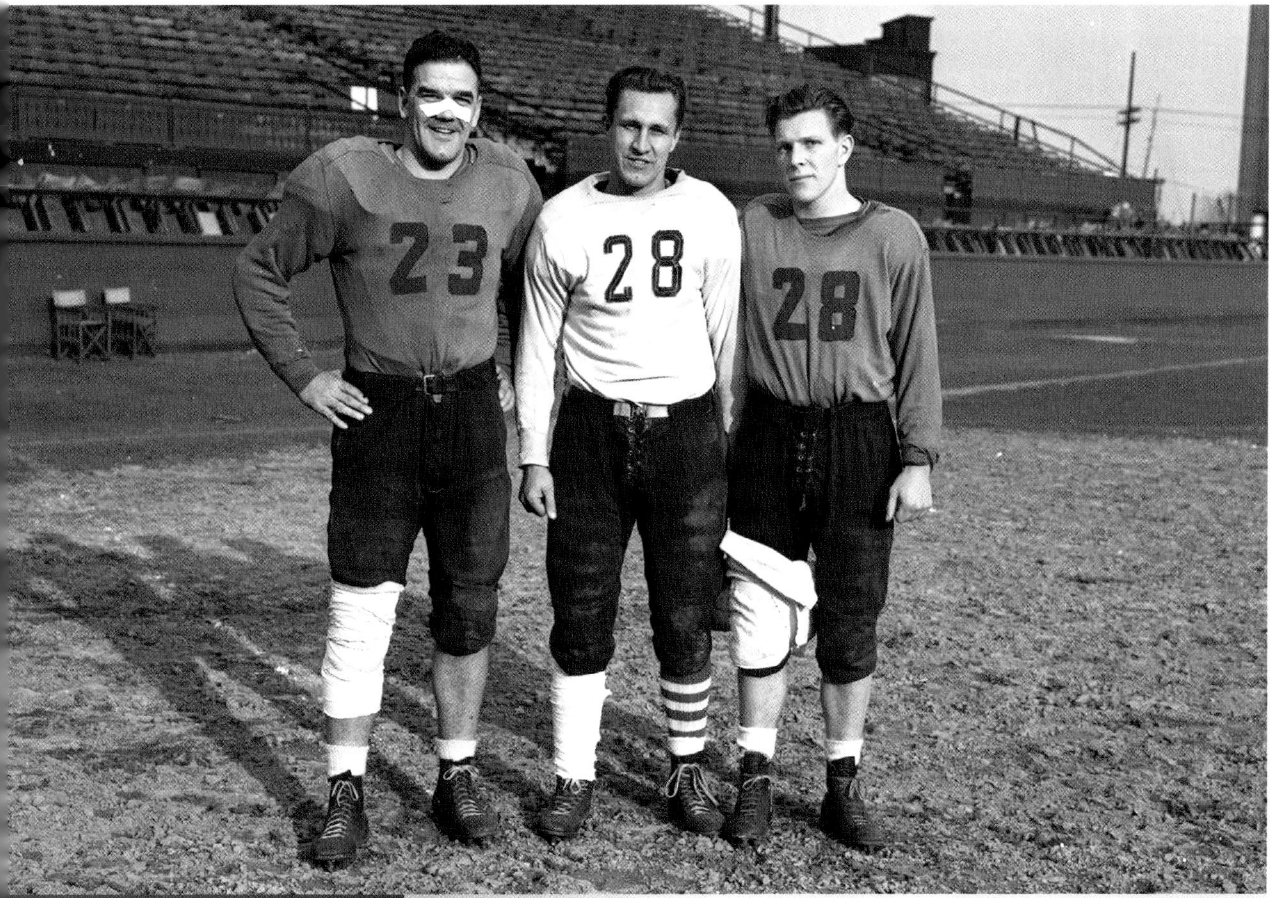
23
28
28

Far left Bob Isbister, 1937-38.

Left Charlie Camilleri snares a pass in the 1946 Grey Cup game.

Bottom middle Frank Morris, 1945-49.

Bottom right Les Ascot, 1940-41 & 1945-53.

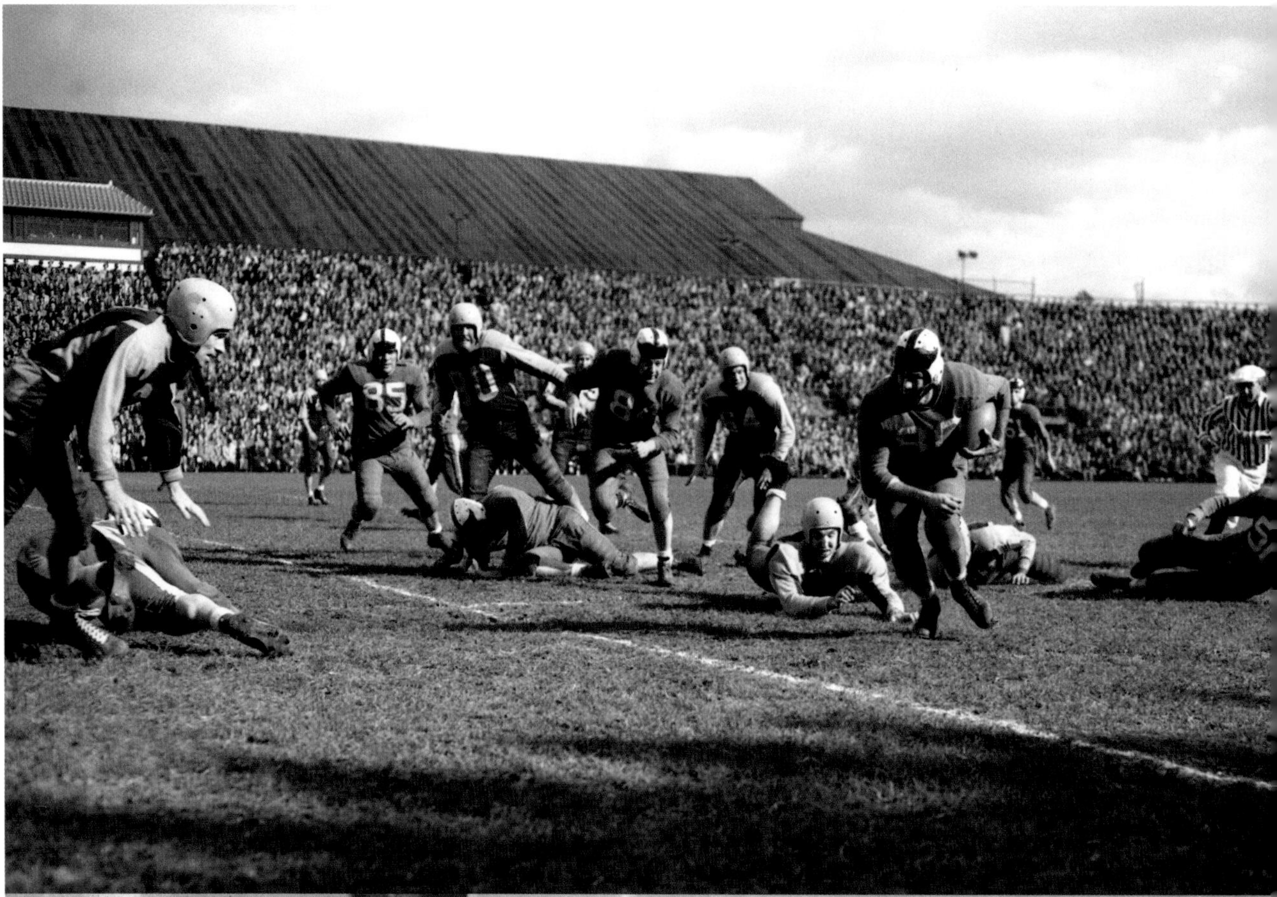

GO!

Left Frank Clair checks out Royal Copeland's abs, 1952.

Above Copeland douses Jake Dunlap, 1949.

Below Argos on the run, left to right, Marv Whaley, Al Dekdebrun, Ulysses Curtis, Doug Smylie, Billy Bass, 1948.

Opposite page, top left Playing defence against Ottawa, 1949.

Opposite page, bottom left Joe Krol ready and rarin' to go!

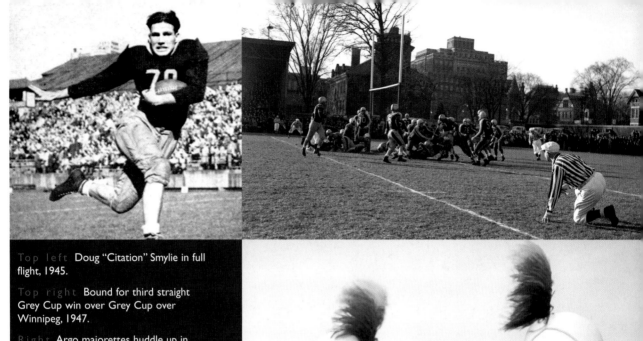

Top left Doug "Citation" Smylie in full flight, 1945.

Top right Bound for third straight Grey Cup win over Grey Cup over Winnipeg, 1947.

Right Argo majorettes huddle up in an unidentified publicity shot from the early '50s.

Below Don Durno (holding) and Fred Doty, 1949.

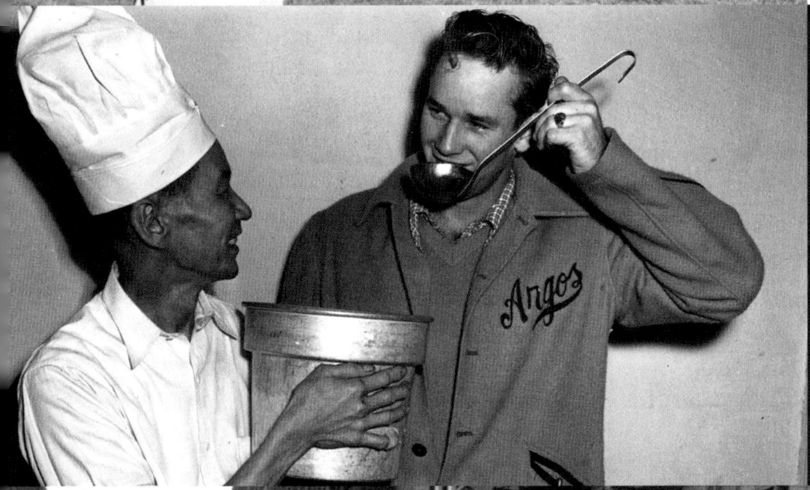

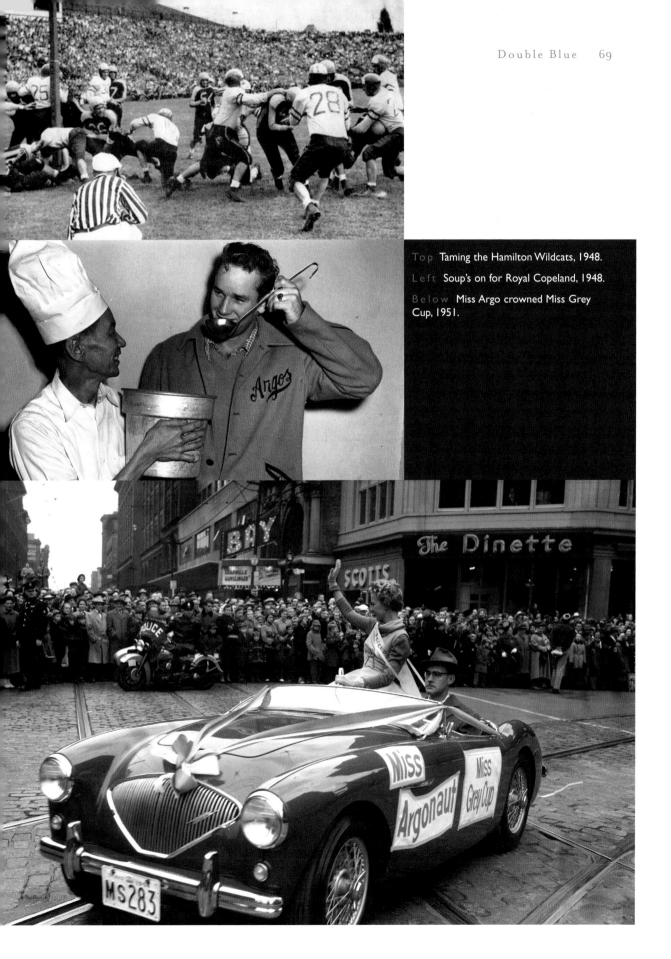

Top Taming the Hamilton Wildcats, 1948.

Left Soup's on for Royal Copeland, 1948.

Below Miss Argo crowned Miss Grey Cup, 1951.

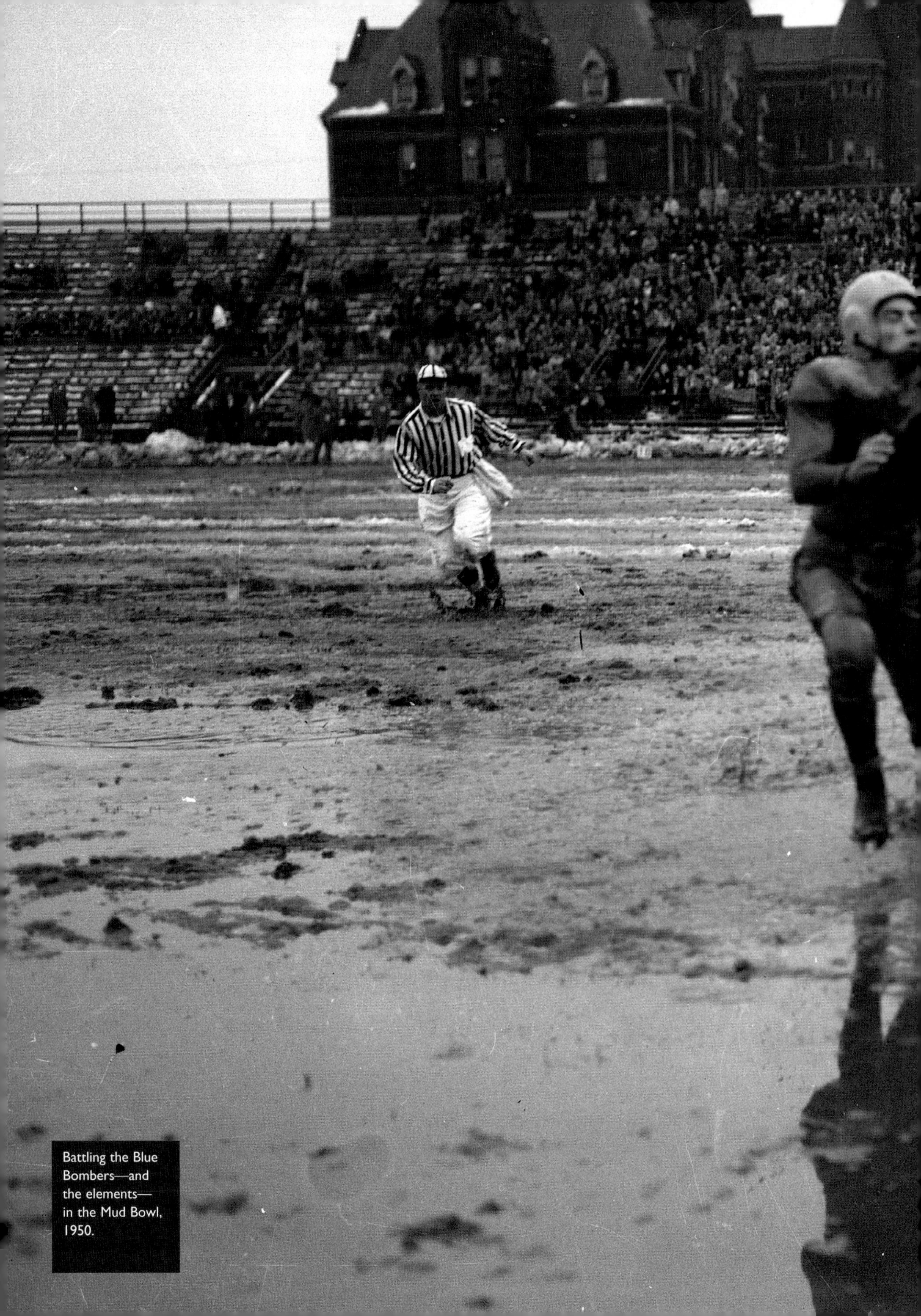

Battling the Blue Bombers—and the elements—in the Mud Bowl, 1950.

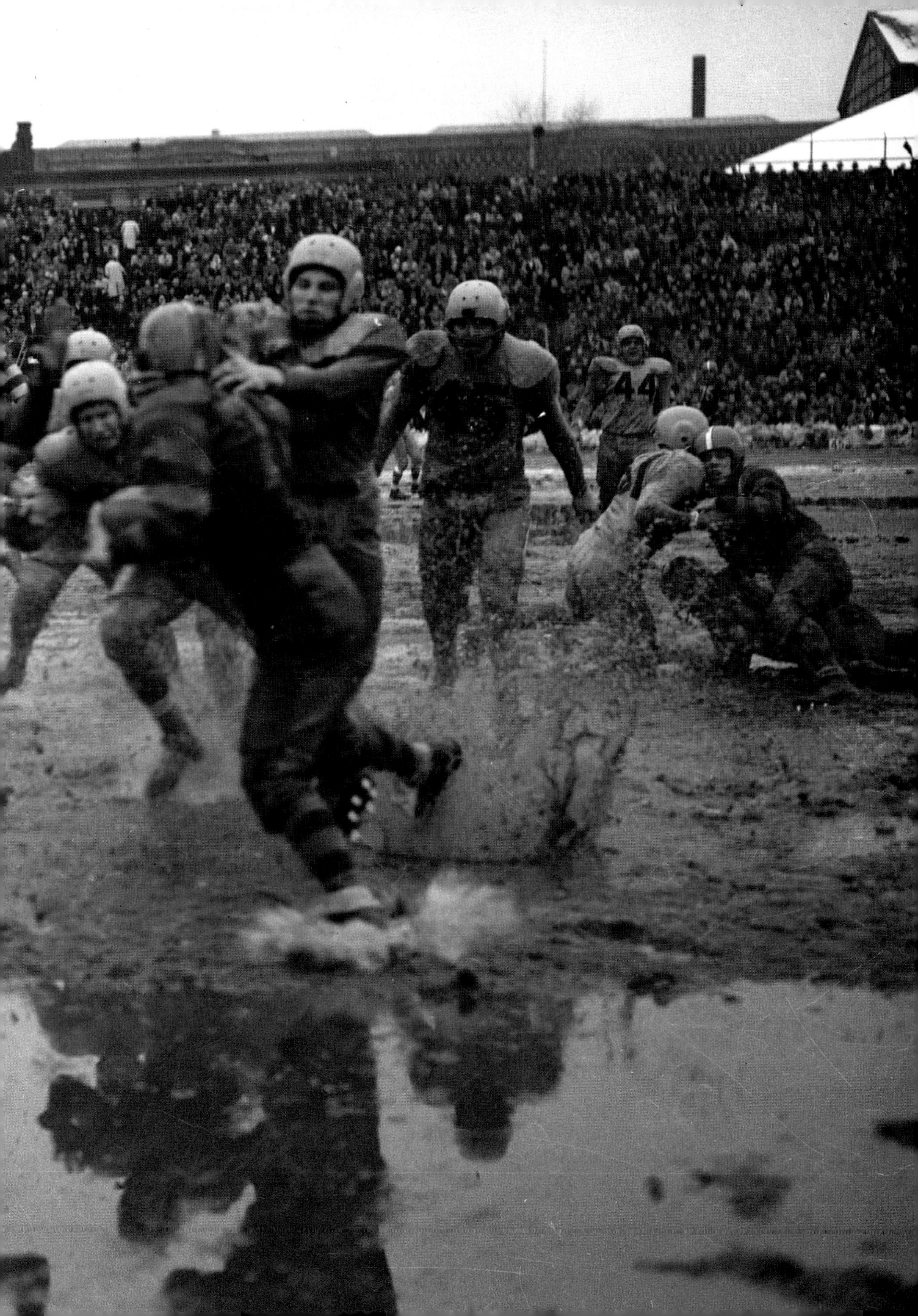

55

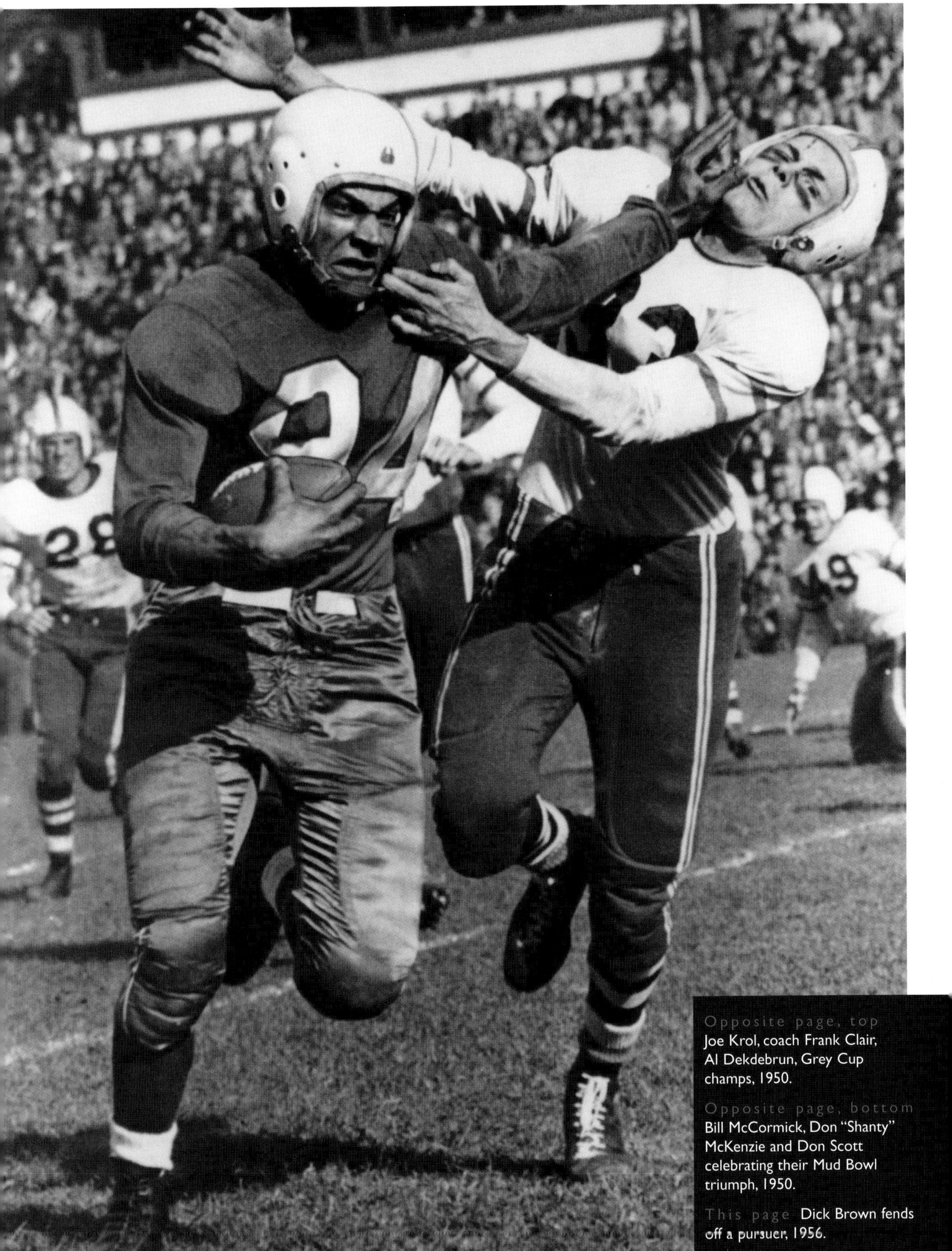

Opposite page, top Joe Krol, coach Frank Clair, Al Dekdebrun, Grey Cup champs, 1950.

Opposite page, bottom Bill McCormick, Don "Shanty" McKenzie and Don Scott celebrating their Mud Bowl triumph, 1950.

This page Dick Brown fends off a pursuer, 1956.

Top Frank Clair, coach, 1950-54.

Top left Don "Red" Ettinger, 1952-53.

Bottom left Pete Bennett, 1948 & 1950-60.

Middle Ed "Buckets" Hirsch, 1950-51.

Lower middle Zeke O'Connor, 1952-53.

Far right top Bob Westlake, 1950-51.

Far right middle Byron Karrys, 1945-51.

Far right bottom Steve Karrys, 1945-46 & 1951-53.

Opposite page, top Taking it to the Eskimos in the Grey Cup game at Varsity Stadium, 1952.

Opposite page, bottom "Red" Ettinger splits the uprights in the same game.

ARGONAUT
EDMONTON
QUARTER
DOWN
YARDS
SWEET CAPS

Above Nobby Wirkowski and friends celebrating their 21-11 Grey Cup win over Edmonton, 1952.

Opposite page
Wirkowski, 1952-54 & 1960.

A drought of 31 years would follow the 1952 Grey Cup victory

80

SECTION 4

4

1953–1972

Dark Ages

If the twentieth century were viewed as a football game, the Toronto Argonauts would be leading at the end of the first half

with a total of nine Grey Cup Championships by 1950. The Boatmen added an unprecedented tenth championship in 1952. The future looked bright for the Argonauts, but unbeknownst at the time, the franchise was about to enter the darkest period in team history.

Prior to 1952, the longest the boys in double blue had gone without a Grey Cup appearance was 11 years (1922-33). The era from 1953-1983, which later became known as The Dark Ages, saw the team go 19 years between Grey Cup appearances and 31 years between Grey Cup victories.

A major reason for the decline in the Argos' fortunes was a league-wide salary cap instituted in 1953. The results were especially damaging to the Argonauts as several players were forced to take salary cuts and subsequently declined to return the ensuing season. The Argonauts finished in the basement for the first time in 40 years.

The Boatmen would make only one more playoff appearance during the 1950s following their Grey Cup win in 1952. Despite the failures of

Left Rod Smylie, 1945-46 & 1948-55.

Right Ticket from an exhibition game against the NFL's Chicago Cardinals on August 15, 1959; It was the first football game played at Exhibition Stadium.

Previous page The long trek back to the home locker room, 1959.

FAN MEMORY

THE SEVEN-YEAR-OLD SHRIMP
BY SHELLY KATES

One of my most cherished memories was when I was seven years old and attended one of my first Argos games with my father at Varsity Stadium.

After the game the players would remain on the field and talk and mingle with the fans. I went down to the field with my Dad and we met Billy Shipp. I was in awe as he shook my hand and talked to us. Here I was, this seven-year-old shrimp talking with this HUGE football player. I probably came up to Billy's thigh! I will be 58 in February and this image is still very vivid in my mind.

Here I was, this seven-year-old shrimp talking with this HUGE football player

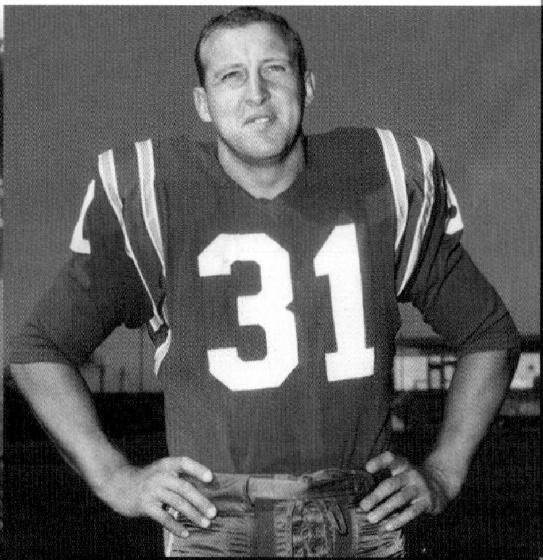

Far left Billy Shipp, 1955-56 & 1961-65.

Left Dick Aldridge, 1965-73.

Right Jim Thorpe, 1969-70.

ARGO MEMORY

LEO CAHILL ON MEL PROFIT

Mel was a leader on our football team and the players and the fans and everybody else looked up to him. The last year Mel was going to be with us, Tony Moro and Bob Hamilton emerged as very capable tight ends. I called Mel in before the season and said, "I don't know how things are going to go, but we have two guys in our Canadian distribution who can play tight end for us. After training camp and when it is all over, you'll probably be the guy who ends up with the job, but it will be a competition." He turned around and walked out of that office and never spoke to me again. Had he stayed he would have played. I guess I was too proud to go running after him. At the Grey Cup, I can remember sitting in the bus with Mel on the way to one practice. I knew he was a leader on the team and I looked to him to be an inspiration in the game. That day we talked about life and things in general. He confided in me that he and his brother were in an orphanage for a while and they had it pretty tough as kids. I felt closeness to him. When I approached him on this thing before training camp and told him we had two guys that were going to compete for that job he just turned around and walked out of my life and the Argonauts' life.

[Mel] turned around and walked out of that office and never spoke to me again

the team, certain individuals were able to achieve some notoriety.

The 1955 team reached the playoffs in large part due to the outstanding duo of quarterback Tom Dublinski and receiver Al Pfeifer. Dublinski, fresh out of the University of Utah, established numerous Argos records in his first season. He certainly earned his league-high salary of more than $17,000 per annum.

Pfeifer, considered one of the greatest receivers to wear double blue, had played one season in 1951 before serving in the Korean War. Upon his return in 1953, Pfeifer had tremendous success with quarterback Al Bruno. With the arrival of Dublinski in 1955, Pfeifer took his game to another level. He led the team with 15 touchdowns in only 12 games and also strung together a streak of six straight games with a touchdown reception that spanned the 1954 and 1955 seasons.

Notwithstanding the individual successes of Dublinski and Pfeifer, the team concluded the season with a record of 4-8, but managed to knock off Hamilton 32-28 in the semi-final. The Argos rolled into Montreal for the East final against the Alouettes in a game that, on paper, they had no chance to win. However, the 1955 squad played a physical game and came up just short in a 38-36 heartbreaker.

Some members of the team, including Dublinski, were so upset by the loss that they stayed in Montreal to drink the night away while the rest of the team returned home to Toronto. Those who remained behind were treated to a healthy dose of local hospitality by a group of sympathetic Montrealers who purchased drinks for the players all night long.

Dublinski suffered a rash of injuries over a couple of seasons as the Argos endured a revolving door at the quarterback position until Tobin Rote emerged to provide some stability. Rote's arrival in 1960, combined with the team's move to the new Exhibition Stadium in 1959, provided a sense of optimism that the double blue would reclaim their status as one of the best football teams in Canada. Rote, a pure passer not known for mobility, is remembered for his heroics on the field and his penchant for the good life off it.

Rote's linemen can fondly recall his ability to drink beer both before and

Some members of the team were so upset by the loss that they stayed in Montreal to drink the night away

Left and above
Ronnie Knox, 1958-59.

Below Head to head with the Alouettes, 1960.

GERRY DOUCETTE JUST GETS OFF A KICK AGAINST THE TICATS, 1957

DICK SHATTO HEADS UPFIELD, 1958

BOBBY KUNTZ BOUND FOR GLORY, 1959

PHIL MUNTZ ELUDES A WOULD-BE TACKLER, 1959

FAN MEMORY

BY DAVID S. HUNTER

My best friend Bob Irwin and I experienced the thrill of meeting Jackie Parker and Sherman Lewis at Exhibition Stadium in 1964. Parker, who passed away in November 2006, had been traded to Toronto from Edmonton in 1963, where he had been a legendary all-purpose player leading the Eskimos to several Grey Cup victories in the 1950s.

Prior to joining the Argos, Lewis had been a two-way All-American halfback at Michigan State, where he was second runner-up for the 1963 Heisman Trophy (behind Roger Staubach, Navy, and Billy Lothridge, Georgia Tech). After leaving the Argos, he played for the New York Jets. Lewis recently retired as offensive coordinator for the Detroit Lions. In the 1990s, he spent time in the same capacity for the Green Bay Packers.

It's interesting to note that Parker, the "fast freight from Mississippi State," and Lewis were successful both offensively and defensively, a rare trait in this day of specialization in sports.

In the attached photo, I am the tall kid with the big ears to the right of Parker. My buddy, Bob Irwin, is the short fellow with the white socks. His father, the late Harvey Irwin, a native of Edmonton, arranged the photo opportunity. Bob, who has been living in England for the past 10 years, and I attended numerous Argos home games in the '60s and retain fond memories of the dynamic Double-Blue.

ARGO MEMORY

JIM ROUNTREE

Steve Owen was an assistant coach with Hamp Poole. He was a real piece of work. He had coached the New York Giants in the '30s at least. He had been with the Giants and won championships. He was just a great guy. We had a great time playing for him in 1959. I was in the secondary and he was coaching the secondary. It was a real treat to have played for him. He was a real legend in the National Football League.

On defence, when the flankers would motion and so forth, we had to decide who was taking the motion when they crossed back and forth. The defensive back who was taking the receiver would say, "I got him" and the guy who was leaving the coverage would say, "You take him."

We were playing Ottawa and that situation arose and Babe Parilli was the quarterback for the Ottawa Rough Riders at the time. As the motion came, Boyd Carter said he had the tight end. The guy that Boyd was supposed to be on went down and caught the TD pass from Parilli.

I came off the field and Coach Steve said, "What happened?"

I said, "Boyd said he had him."

And Steve said, "Don't listen to Boyd, he'll lie to you."

It was hysterical. We were trying to win the game and Boyd's going to lie to me.

after practice. And Rote made sure to take good care of his linemen. When he first arrived in Toronto, Rote proclaimed that he would take his offensive line to dinner for each game he went untouched. As lineman Fred Black once stated, "He was the best protected quarterback in Argo history."

Rote built a strong chemistry with Dave Mann, one of the greatest all-round players in the history of the game. Together they led the Argonauts back to the top of their division for the first time since 1937, compiling a record of 10-4.

Rote had a magical season in 1960. He threw seven touchdown passes in a game against Montreal twice in the same month—on October 1, 1960 in a 50-15 win at Exhibition Stadium and again at home on October 30, 1960 in a 63-27 victory.

Two months earlier, on August 19 against Montreal, Rote established an Argonauts club record of 524 yards passing in one game, which still stands to this day. Rote also remains atop the records books in Toronto for his 108-yard TD pass to Jim Rountree against Saskatchewan on

ARGO MEMORY

JIM ROUNTREE ON HIS ARGO RECORD 108-YARD TOUCHDOWN RECEPTION

Tobin (Rote) and I had a lot of good times. I was playing mostly defence, but I lived at the same place where Tobin lived on Jarvis Street. A few ballplayers lived in there and we used to walk over to practice together every day.

Tobin was a great guy. He was a great football player.

I was glad to have had the opportunity to play with him and make that big play.

It was September 10, 1961. We were on our two-yard line going from east to west. I was on the offensive left side of the formation, the south side of the stadium at the CNE. It was a quick slant pattern and Tobin hit me and I just took it up the opposite sideline 108 yards for the touchdown.

When I came off the field I was worn out. I was playing offence and defence. I missed the next two series of downs. The coach, Lou Agase, walks over to me and says, "Hey Jim, we appreciate the touchdown, but are you going to play anymore?"

That's been 40-something years and I will never forgot what he said to me.

Top left Jackie Parker (12), Sherman Lewis and fans, Exhibition Stadium, 1964.

Far left A weary Rountree jogs off the field after his record romp, 1961.

Left Tobin Rote, 1960-62.

September 10, 1961.

Toronto had two great chances to reach the Grey Cup during the Rote years. But in 1960 the Argonauts were foiled in the Eastern final by an Ottawa Rough Riders' sleeper play executed perfectly by Bobby Simpson. Then the following year, the Argonauts blew an 18-point first-game lead in the second game of a two-game total point semi-final series to their hated rivals from Hamilton.

By the mid-1960s, the Argos' fortunes remained dark

By the mid-1960s, the Argos' fortunes remained dark. Head Coach Lou Agase led the team to an 0-3 record out of the gate and he was replaced by a former Argonauts star player, Nobby Wirkowski. But Wirkowski failed to make the playoffs. Bob Shaw replaced Wirkowski at the start of the 1965 season and promptly led the Argos to back-to-back last place finishes.

From 1962-1966, the team finished last in the East Division five consecutive seasons, leaving the Argonauts the distinction of having the worst record in all of Canadian football in that span with a mark of 19-51.

One of the lone bright spots of the era was the legendary Dick Shatto. The team's best player and most recognized personality, he could do just about everything on the football field. Arguably, Shatto was the Argonaut franchise during the early years of The Dark Ages. He lived in Toronto all year round and he became entrenched in the community. He truly was an Argonaut through and through. Shatto eventually became the General Manager of the team, but unfortunately he never won a Grey Cup during his time as a player. It is striking that in spite of playing 159 league games, Shatto only appeared in seven playoff games and never played in a Grey Cup championship.

There was renewed optimism in the spring of 1967 when Lew Hayman called a press conference and announced the signing of Leo Cahill as the new head coach—the fourth of the decade. Cahill, previously head coach of the cross-town Toronto Rifles of the Continental League, injected the Argonauts with an "us-against-them" mentality and stoked hope among the Argonauts faithful. Prior to Cahill's arrival, the grandstand at Exhibition Stadium would be half empty. But Cahill was a great marketer

ARGO MEMORY

PETE MARTIN ON DICK SHATTO VS. BOB SHAW

Bob Shaw used to fine us all the time. We weren't making a heck of a lot of money back then. We used to get our pay cheques at the first practice after a game. We had to line up and if Shaw was going to fine you he withheld your pay cheque. You would have to write him a cheque for the fine before he would give you your pay cheque.

One time in 1965 he fined Dick Shatto. It was Shatto's last year and he was our best player by far. He always showed up to play, but Shaw fined him for 'indifferent play.' He and Bob Shaw hated each other.

As the story goes, we were all lined up and Dick grabbed his pay cheque, endorsed it and threw it right back at Shaw and said, "Keep the whole thing."

Above Dick Shatto, 1954-65.

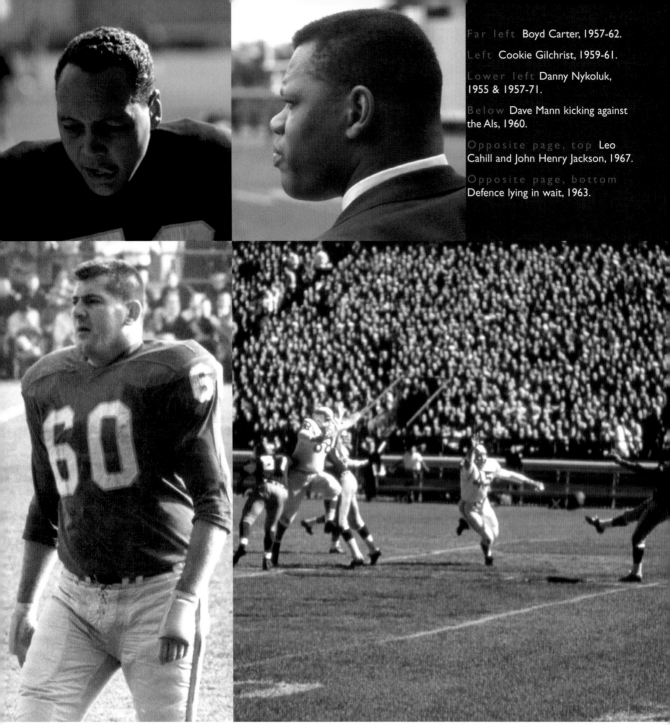

Far left Boyd Carter, 1957-62.

Left Cookie Gilchrist, 1959-61.

Lower left Danny Nykoluk, 1955 & 1957-71.

Below Dave Mann kicking against the Als, 1960.

Opposite page, top Leo Cahill and John Henry Jackson, 1967.

Opposite page, bottom Defence lying in wait, 1963.

Cahill stoked hope among the Argonauts faithful

ARGOS
TORONTO
TORONTO

FAN MEMORY

BY AARON CARR

We had season tickets from the late '60s to the late '70s. I will always cherish the time I spent with my Dad and brothers. It was about the time that the famous Argo cheer "Argooos" started as well as the "Argo Bounce." My favourite year was 1971, the first time the Argos had made the Grey Cup final in a long time. It was the year they had all of the "star" players. I never had given up hope during the Grey Cup game. From Harry Abofs' unintentional kick out of bounds, Tricky Dick's interception and the heart-breaker—Leon "X Ray" McQuay's fumble.

From then on it was downhill especially with the chants of "Goodbye Leo." All in all the Argos have always been my favourite sports team in any sport.

Right Leon "X-Ray" McQuay, 1971-73 & 1977.

ARGO MEMORY

PETE MARTIN

We were in Calgary and Neil Armstrong was going to step on the moon. We had a game the next day.

Tom Wilkinson was my roommate. He was the big story and I was like his road secretary. We would check into the room and the first thing he would do is turn on the TV set. Then he would take the pillow from the head of the bed and put it at the foot of the bed, go get the garbage can and put the garbage can at the foot of the bed, go get his chewing tobacco and spit into the can and watch TV.

The phone would ring and media would want interviews so I would arrange interviews for him.

Leo Cahill wanted to practise that day. We said, "Leo, they're gonna put a man on the moon for crying out loud." We talked him out of going to practise.

Wilkie and I sat in our room at the Palliser Hotel and watched Neil Armstrong step on the moon. It was one of those things where you always remember where you are in key situations.

Left Peter Martin, 1965-72.

and the season ticket base rose from roughly 13,500 to 29,000. By 1971, the team was playing in front of sellout crowds.

It didn't take Cahill long to accomplish his first goal—the Argonauts finished third in the East Division and returned to the playoffs for the first time since 1961.

In addition to becoming a success on the field, the Argos were also becoming a rough-and-tumble crew that included the likes of Bill Frank, Bobby Taylor, Marv Luster, Mel Profit, and Dick Thornton. The "Renegades," as they were affectionately known, spent many hours at The Jarvis House, a local watering hole. It was a ritual to gather there following the first practice of a new week. The guys would toss their bonus money from the previous game onto the table and drink together as a team until the pot disappeared.

"By 1971, it was almost a mandatory thing," recalled running back Bill Symons. "We were a very close team. It was probably the best team I played on, other than when I was in high school. We kept everybody together: defence and offence."

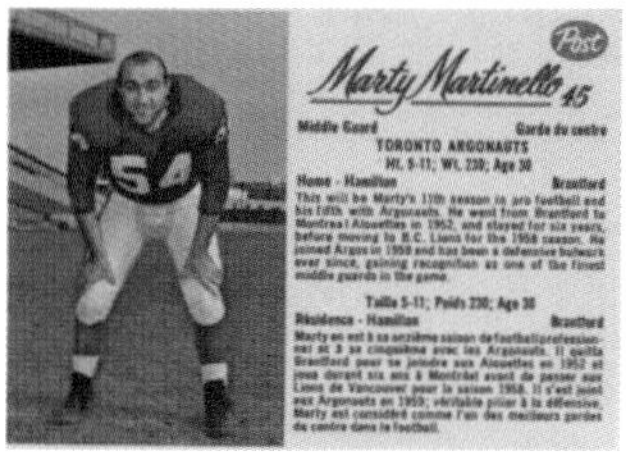

Marty Martinello, 1959-65.

Symons, a little-known running back when he was acquired from the B.C. Lions, blossomed in his second year with the Boatmen, 1968, becoming the first Argo to rush for 1,000 yards in a season (1,107 yards) and becoming the first player in franchise history to capture the Schenley Award as CFL player of the year .

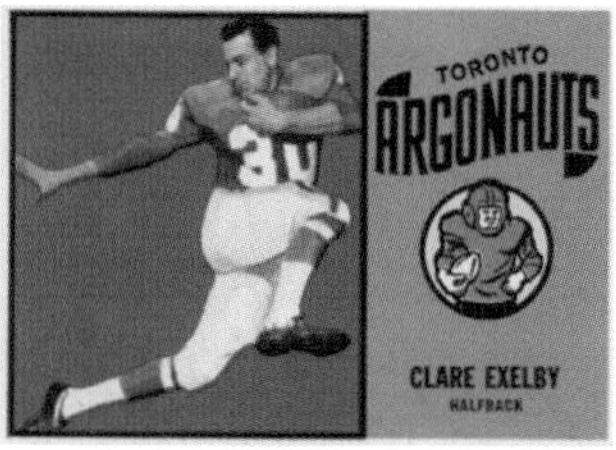

Clare Exelby, 1958-59 & 1961-63.

According to most, that memorable 1968 season produced the defining moment to announce that Cahill's crew had truly arrived. The date was November 9 and the scene was Exhibition Stadium against the hated Tiger-Cats in the East Division semi-final. The Tiger-Cats had exploded to a 14-0 lead and had the Argos pinned deep in their own territory. Toronto quarterback Wally Gabler handed the ball off to Symons, who found space off tackle to the right behind a pair of big blocks from Charlie Bray and Jim Dillard. Symons escaped to the outside, squared his shoulders downfield and outran the entire Tiger-Cats squad to the endzone.

"You talk about one play turning the whole thing around," recalled

Peter Martin. "The place was going nuts."

The touchdown energized the Argos and they went on to knock off Hamilton before going down to defeat at the hands of the eventual Grey Cup champion Ottawa Rough Riders in the East Division final.

By 1969, the lore of the "Renegades" continued to grow. Dave Raimey was added to the team along with Chip Barrett in exchange for quarterback Wally Gabler. While team owner John Bassett disagreed with Cahill's trade, the move sparked the team and the Argonauts finished with a record of 10-4.

Once again, the Boatmen took out the Tiger-Cats in the semi-final, setting up another showdown with Ottawa for a chance to play for the Grey Cup. Led by quarterback Tom Wilkinson, playing with a sore shoulder, the Argos took a 22-14 lead to Ottawa for the second game in the two-game total-points series. Everything was rolling according to plan until Leo Cahill's uttered his infamous comment: "It will take an act of God to beat us on Saturday."

God must have been a Russ Jackson fan. On a day the legendary quarterback was honoured in what became his final CFL game at home, the heavens opened up and left the field covered in ice. The Ottawa players were prepared for the weather and wore broomball shoes. The Argos players spent the day slipping and sliding all over the place as their Grey Cup hopes were dashed in a 32-3 loss.

Ed Harrington, 1963-65, 1967-71 & 1974.

The 1970 season brought another second-place finish combined with a disappointing playoff loss—this time to the Montreal Alouettes. But entering the 1971 season the Argonauts believed their time had finally arrived. Leo Cahill was at his best during the off-season, signing several American stars, including Joe Theismann, Leon McQuay, Greg Barton, Jim Stillwagon and Gene Mack. Zenon Andrusyshyn was brought in from UCLA to become the team's new kicker.

To make room for the newcomers, some veterans were either traded or released, including quarterbacks Tom Wilkinson and Don Jonas, who would each become the CFL's Most Outstanding Player in different uniforms. A new team nucleus was created around Theismann and

ARGO MEMORY

LEO CAHILL ON LEON MCQUAY

I always tell people that when Leon slipped I fell. You know, as far as Leon was concerned, we wouldn't have been within 2,000 miles of Vancouver (the Grey Cup game) without him.

Leon had great strength and great speed, but he was a problem. He came out of an area in Florida that was just a bad place to be raised. I remember when I recruited him one of the questions he asked was if it was OK for him to go to the grocery store and shop.

I said, "What the hell are you talking about? Toronto is a safe place and they'll love you there."

The players thought I gave him special treatment. One thing that the players didn't know was that Leon had tremendously high blood pressure. During the practice sessions he would say, "Coach I can taste blood." And I would tell him to go and sit down for a couple of minutes.

Leon wasn't Mr. Personality with the rest of the players. He was very quiet and very inward and that caused some problems with the other guys as far as that was concerned.

I still think Leon was one of the greatest football talents I ever saw.

Right Leon McQuay.

Below Bill Symons, 1967-73.

ARGO MEMORY

BILL SYMONS ON HIS CFL PLAYOFF RECORD 100-YARD TD RUN

There was a sold-out crowd at Exhibition Stadium on November 9, 1968, and we were getting our butts kicked by Hamilton. We were stunned because we were down 14-0. We were on our own 10-yard line and it was a straight off tackle play to the right. I was the left halfback and Jimmy Dillard was the right halfback. Wally Gabler handed the ball off to me and I just followed big Charlie Bray. Dillard got a good block and Bobby Taylor got a great block.

After that, it was just a foot race. I never got touched and there were no great moves. There was no mystery on that play.

I've always felt that I've had a lot better plays, where you hit somebody and five or six guys have to bring you down and you get an extra ten yards. It's more gratifying if you try to run over somebody to make some extra yardage than to have a foot race.

It's more gratifying if you try to run over somebody

FAN MEMORY

BY WALLACE PIDGEON

My favourite memory is not about a play, player, coach, game, or even a stadium that the Argonauts have played in. It is about a man.

This man worked two jobs for 30 years, put food on our table, a roof over our heads, somehow found a way to buy Argonauts season tickets and shared his passion for the Double Blue.

He introduced me to the Argos in 1971—the year of Theismann, McQuay, Cahill and the greatest team to never win the Grey Cup.

He would talk about the magic of Varsity Stadium, the chemistry of Krol and Copeland—the Gold Dust Twins—the grace of Uly Curtis, the power of Cookie Gilchrist, his disdain for Lew Hayman, the swiftness of Dick Shatto and the pride in an organization for hiring Willie Wood—the very first head coach of colour in football.

Huddled in Exhibition Stadium on the 55-yard line, 52 rows up in the old grandstand, we watched Davis, Metcalf and the powder blue uniforms come and go, while waiting for a Grey Cup to come back to our city.

Now a season ticket holder myself, the love for the Canadian game, the team and tradition that is as much a part of me as the double blue that runs through my veins is due to the man I sat beside for over 20 years game in and game out. And I am planning on attending the 95th Grey Cup this year with my football hero—my dad—Don Pidgeon.

ARGO MEMORY

LEO CAHILL ON JOE THEISMANN

One of the things that I remember most was the Joe Theismann story from 1971. He had committed to the Miami Dolphins. We had recruited him, too. We had gone to South Bend, Indiana and saw him practice and play a few times.

In the final analysis, he was drafted by the Dolphins. They had a big press conference announcing that he had agreed to play with Miami.

Joe had been up to visit us before so I knew him and his wife. I called him and I wished him lots of luck with the Dolphins. He said to me, "Wait just a minute coach; I have the contract in my back pocket right now. I haven't signed anything."

Joe wanted to talk to his college coach before he signed it.

I invited him and his wife back up here for one more trip. We gave him the full course treatment and signed him up here. I haven't had many more Christmas cards from Don Shula since then.

Left and above Joe Theismann, 1971-73.

Barton at quarterback, Stillwagon, Jim Corrigall, McQuay and Paul Desjardins. Long-serving lineman Danny Nykoluk retired while Bobby Taylor was released, in part due to the return of Mike Eben who had been loaned to the Edmonton Eskimos the previous year in a bizarre arrangement orchestrated by Cahill.

Dick Thornton, 1967-72.

Mike Wadsworth, 1966-70.

Cahill's off-season moves paid dividends as the Argonauts finished atop the East Division for the first time since 1960. Theismann won the Eastern Football Conference passing title while McQuay, despite being injured for part of the season, emerged as one of the best running backs in the CFL, placing runner-up to ex-Argo Don Jonas as the CFL Player of the Year. For his efforts, Cahill was named the Coach of the Year.

The success on the field brought success at the gate. Every home game in 1971 was a sellout. The official number of fans announced at Exhibition Stadium each game was 33,135—an increase of more than 10,000 fans per game since the arrival of Cahill.

"I remember 33,135 coming to the CNE almost every weekend," recalled the late Dick Aldridge. "When you walked down the street, everyone knew you."

After a 19-year drought, the 1971 Argonauts marched into the 59th Grey Cup game against the Calgary Stampeders at Empire Stadium in Vancouver. The game was a defensive struggle in which the Argonauts never held the lead, but did have chances to win the game. The best chance came in the fourth quarter by way of a Dick Thornton interception return that took the ball to the Calgary 11-yard line with the Argonauts trailing 14-11. On the next play, McQuay took a pitchout and ran to the right side. He was quickly tackled by Dick Suderman. On second down the Argos went back to McQuay. This time it was a sweep around the left end. McQuay slipped. He was hit by defensive back Larry Robinson. The ball was loose on the turf and Frank Andruski recovered it for the Stampeders.

"When he fumbled the ball, I think everybody was more ticked off than if Sy (Bill Symons) had fumbled it," said Peter Martin. "I think it wouldn't have been as big of a deal. But when Leon fumbled it, it became a big deal. It was because of his practice habits and his moods; there wasn't the forgiveness there that would have been there if Sy was there."

Leon McQuay was painted as the scapegoat for the Argonauts' plight, but the Toronto defence forced Calgary to go two-and-out on the ensuing series to give the Argos one last chance. But the Stampeders' punt landed near Argos returner Harry Abofs and the wet ball caromed off his foot and out of bounds. As a result of the football exiting the field off Abofs' foot, a little-known rule was invoked that awarded Calgary the ball.

"When he kicked that ball out of bounds that was a bigger tragedy than the fumble," said Symons. "Heck, I've been a running back long enough to know that you can fumble any time. Why Harry kicked that out, I'll never know."

The Argos eventually regained possession of the football on their own 28-yard line with time for one final play. It was too little, too late and the Argos' hopes of winning the Grey Cup were erased.

Leo Cahill summed it up with one of his most famous quotes, "Leon McQuay slipped and I fell."

The Cahill era began to disintegrate following the '71 season. Toronto had been the odds-on favourite to win the Grey Cup in 1972, but those hopes began to fade when Theismann broke his leg in the second quarter of the season opener. In short order the Argos resembled a M.A.S.H. unit. Martin, McQuay, Raimey, Corrigall, Tim Anderson, Ed Harrington, John Trainor—the injury list went on and on and on.

The Argos came to the final game of the regular season needing to beat Hamilton. But they lost and, for the first time since 1966, the proud men of the blue on blue finished dead last and missed the playoffs.

The following Thursday morning at 10 o'clock Cahill was summoned to the office of team owner John Bassett. In the company of President Lew Hayman, Bassett told Cahill he was fired, thus ending the Leo Cahill era.

With Cahill's exit, the Argonauts found themselves in the same position as the team that stumbled back in 1953 under Frank Clair. And it would be another decade before the gloomy cloud of The Dark Ages would dissipate.

~ JAIME STEIN

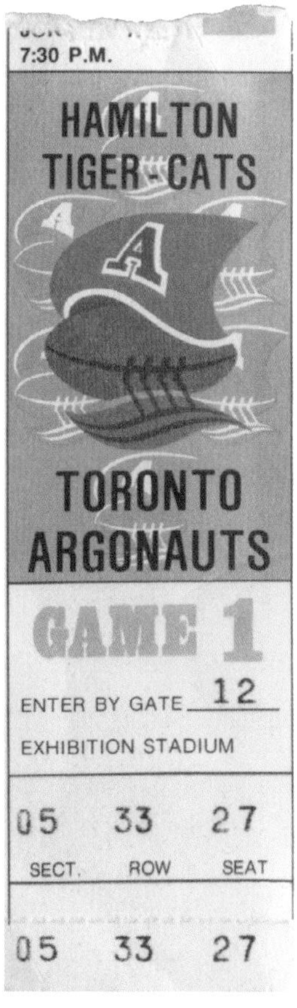

Images
1953–1972

Ron Brewer, 1958-60 & 1963-65.

ARGO

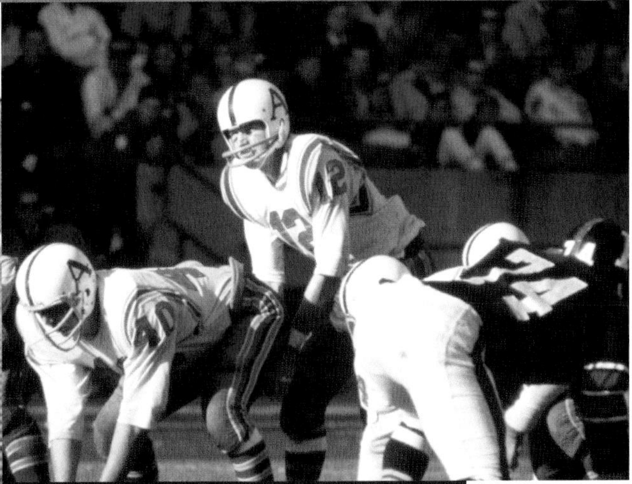

Top School's in under Bob Shaw, 1966.

Left Marv Luster, 1964-72.

Above Wally Gabler barking signals, 1968.

Opposite page, top left
Jackie Parker, 1963-65.

Opposite page, top right
Wally Gabler, 1966-69 & 1972.

Opposite page, bottom left
Eagle Day hauled down, 1966.

Opposite page, bottom right
Head coach Bob Shaw (centre) with assistants Bob Dennis and Gord Ackerman, 1965.

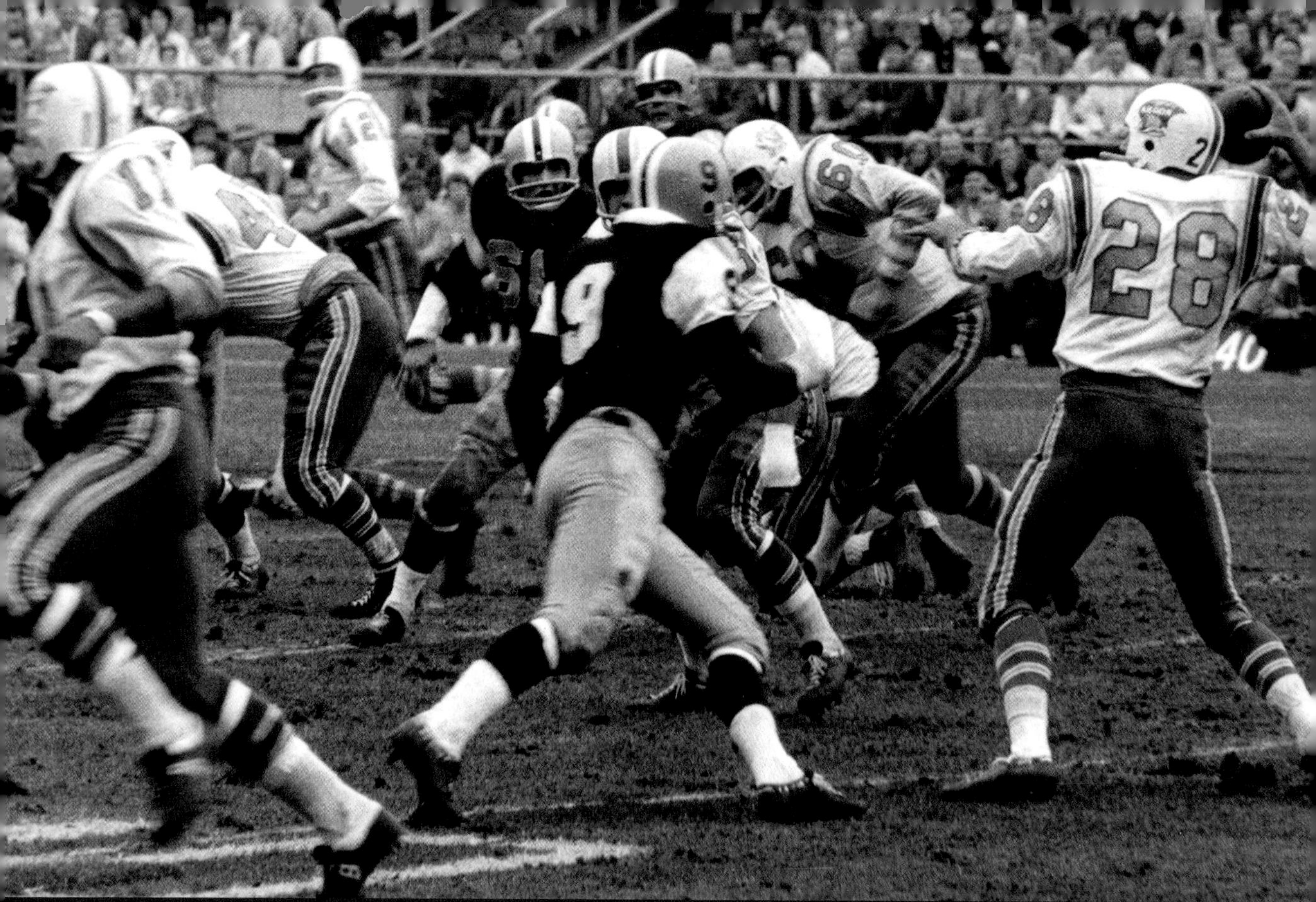

JACKIE PARKER UNDER PRESSURE, 1964

BILL SYMONS GROUNDED BY THE ALS, 1968

DAVE THELEN ON THE MOVE, 1966

DICKIE MOORE LUNGING AHEAD, 1969

Top Dick Shatto losing his grip, 1961.

Below Dick Fouts, 1957-61 & 1967.

Bottom right Mel Profit, Dave Mann and a model pose for a photo shoot, 1969.

Opposite page, top left Tony Moro signs on the dotted line for Leo Cahill, 1970.

Opposite page, top right An injured Dick Shatto, 1961.

Opposite page, middle right Norm Stoneburgh, 1955-58 & 1960-67.

Opposite page, bottom Dave Mann becomes a Canadian citizen.

A

40

HOLY BIBLE

Pete Martin
(centre), Mel
Profit and the rest
of the Argo team
get psyched.

Top Bobby Taylor, 1966-70 & 1974.

Below Bill Symons grinding it out, 1971.

Bottom Dave Raimey, 1969-74.

Opposite page, left A young Tom Wilkinson, 1968.

Opposite page, top right "Wilkie" pitching to Raimey, 1969.

Opposite page, bottom right Jim Corrigall, 1970-81.

And it would be another decade before the gloomy cloud of The Dark Ages would dissipate

AFTER a hiatus of nearly two decades, the Miss Argo contest was resurrected in 2006. Herewith, a tribute to one of the grand traditions of Canadian football between the early 1950s and late '80s. Although the criteria varied over the years, the applicants, aspiring to represent their city in the Miss Grey Cup Pageant, generally had to be single, between the ages of 17 and 22 and with no professional modelling experience.

1957

1959

1961

MISS ARGONAUT '61

MISS
ARGONAUT
1963

ARGONAUT 1969

Parade at Last

5

1973–1990

SECTION 5

ARGOS
CHAMPIONS
5
TORONTO ARGONAUTS

TORONTO ARGONAUTS

The long drought was finally over. In the thunderous din of the newly-opened

B.C. Place Stadium, on a November day in 1983, the Argonauts ended 31 years of heartbreaks, frustration and bitter disappointments when they defeated the hometown Lions 18-17 to hoist the Grey Cup for first time since 1952.

Condredge Holloway, who a year earlier had been named the CFL's most outstanding player but was unable to bring Earl Grey's mug back to Toronto, led the Argos to a then-club-record 12-4 during the regular season. However, weakened by the flu during Grey Cup week, he struggled in the championship game and gave way to backup Joe Barnes, who had been effective in relief at various times during the season.

The Argos were trailing 17-12 late in the fourth quarter when Barnes entered the game and drove the team to the B.C. Lions' five-yard line. He then lofted a soft pass in the flats to running back Cedric Minter, who had little trouble sprinting the short distance to the end zone. While their attempt at a two-point convert failed, the Argos hung on for the victory. The Cup was finally back in T.O.

But we're getting ahead of ourselves.

The road to that long-elusive championship began in 1973. That was less than a year after Argo fans' derisive chants of "Goodbye Leo" had

Left Finally, a City Hall reception; Metro Toronto Chairman Paul Godfrey and Toronto Mayor Art Eggleton flanking club president Ralph Sazio, chairman Rod McInnes and head coach Bob O'Billovich.

Previous page Condredge Holloway, 1981-86.

heralded Leo Cahill's departure, not knowing that there would be a second coming of the controversial coach just five years later. It was a memorable era of highs and lows ending in 1989 with the firing of Bob O'Billovich, who to this day, is the winningest coach in the club's history.

The days between Cahill's initial departure and O'Billovich's arrival in 1982 were without a doubt nine of the most tumultuous years in the club's turbulent history. It was also a time when Toronto sports fans loved to hate the Argos. Crowds that later owners could only dream of filled Exhibition Stadium as the Boatmen sailed from one disastrous outcome to another.

It was also a time when Toronto sports fans loved to hate the Argos

"We didn't win a lot of games, but we filled Exhibition Stadium," recalled all-star defensive tackle Granville Liggins, whom the Argos had pried away from the Calgary Stampeders in 1972. "We had three or four or five different quarterbacks and how many coaches?"

Nine, Granny, nine. A seemingly endless string of coaches hollered and screamed, cajoled and pleaded, but to little avail as the team mustered just one winning season from 1972 through 1981. That was in '73 when they finished 7-5-2 under John Rauch before losing to Montreal in the East final.

That would be the final year for Joe Theismann, whose signing in 1971 had created much buzz in the U.S. as well as Canada. Joe The Throw would jump to the NFL before the '74 season, but by the midway point of the '73 season, with the team struggling at a 3-4 pace, Rauch was gone.

"Rauch had a tough time adapting to the Canadian game," said Canadian receiver Mike Eben, one of the most cerebral players to ever play in the league. A University of Toronto graduate, Eben continued his post-grad work while playing for the Argos.

"Rauch came up from the Oakland Raiders and he had very fixed ideas. I think he didn't feel Canadians could play the game that much."

With Rauch's firing the parade of head coaches began. Assistant Joe Moss filled in after Rauch's firing, but he was not re-hired the next season. Instead, owner Bill Hodgson, who had bought the team from media mogul John Bassett a year earlier, brought in CFL legend Russ Jackson, the Hall of Fame Ottawa Rough Rider quarterback, even though

Left Granville Liggins, 1972-78.

Above Jim Stillwagon, 1971-75.

Below Head coach Russ Jackson (1975-76) and Doyle Orange (1974-76).

There I was, standing next to head coach Rauch, with rapidly melting ice cream streaming down my face

ARGO MEMORY

MIKE EBEN

John Rauch, formerly of the Oakland Raiders of the NFL, was coaching the Argos in the 1973 season and having a difficult time of it to be sure. The CFL was a dramatically different game to that of the NFL. Rauch had brought along with him all of the notions of that league south of the border, not realizing that he had to contend with a Canadian breed of player, import rules, different game rules and, all in all, a somewhat independent mentality which he had never before encountered.

We were losing badly in Regina during a late July prairie heat-wave. Rauch, a big man, was sweating on a number of counts. Suddenly the whole stadium was enveloped in darkness—a flash storm had struck the electrical system of Taylor Field and although there seemed to be no rain, the game was halted as it was pitch black. We all just sat there, doing and seeing nothing, but boiling hot in our sweaty uniforms. During the uncanny silence, I kept hearing the constant barking of an ice cream boy who insisted on plying his wares. Well, at this juncture of the game, the idea of a refreshing ice was most appealing, so I set about to find this fellow to see if I would be able to secure one of his cool creams. I went up into the stands, not with out difficulty—it was black after all—and finally found the lad who was willing to sell me an ice upon promise of reimbursement at the end of the game. A deal was struck and I soon found myself back by the bench on the playing field, happily lapping away at my recently-acquired ice cream bar. Suddenly the lights came back on and there I was, standing next to head coach Rauch, with rapidly melting ice cream streaming down my face and Argo uniform. Rauch turned and looked at me, was about to utter a holler of dismay, despair, whatever but managed to gather himself and strode off without a word. The whole episode seemed to sum up the game day. We were soundly thrashed and I am sure that John Rauch's lasting image of that particular loss was the vision of his wide receiver Eben standing next to him covered in melted vanilla and chocolate ice cream. So went that season of '73!

Jackson had no coaching experience. The result was predictable. After two unsuccessful seasons Jackson returned to being an educator.

The Argos' ineptness on the field was frustrating for the fans as the team was not devoid of talent. Theismann wasn't the only U.S. college star to be lured into a Double Blue jersey with a sizeable contract. He was followed north by the likes of Ohio State stars Jim Stillwagon and Tim Anderson, and Memphis State's Eric Harris. They also talked Barrie, Ontario native Jim Corrigall, who starred at Kent State, into signing with them rather than the St. Louis Cardinals, who had chosen him in the second round of the 1970 NFL draft.

The most heralded signing after Theismann was undoubtedly that of former USC star and 1974 Heisman Trophy runner-up Anthony Davis, who became the CFL's first $1-million signing. But the arrogant Davis, who was shunned by his teammates, left after just one season bearing the tag as one of the club's biggest flops ever.

Jackson's firing paved the way for the return of Cahill to the Boatmen. His second term in the wheelhouse was a lot shorter, but just as turbulent.

Left
Mike Eben, 1968-69 & 1971-77.

Below
Peter Muller, 1973-81.

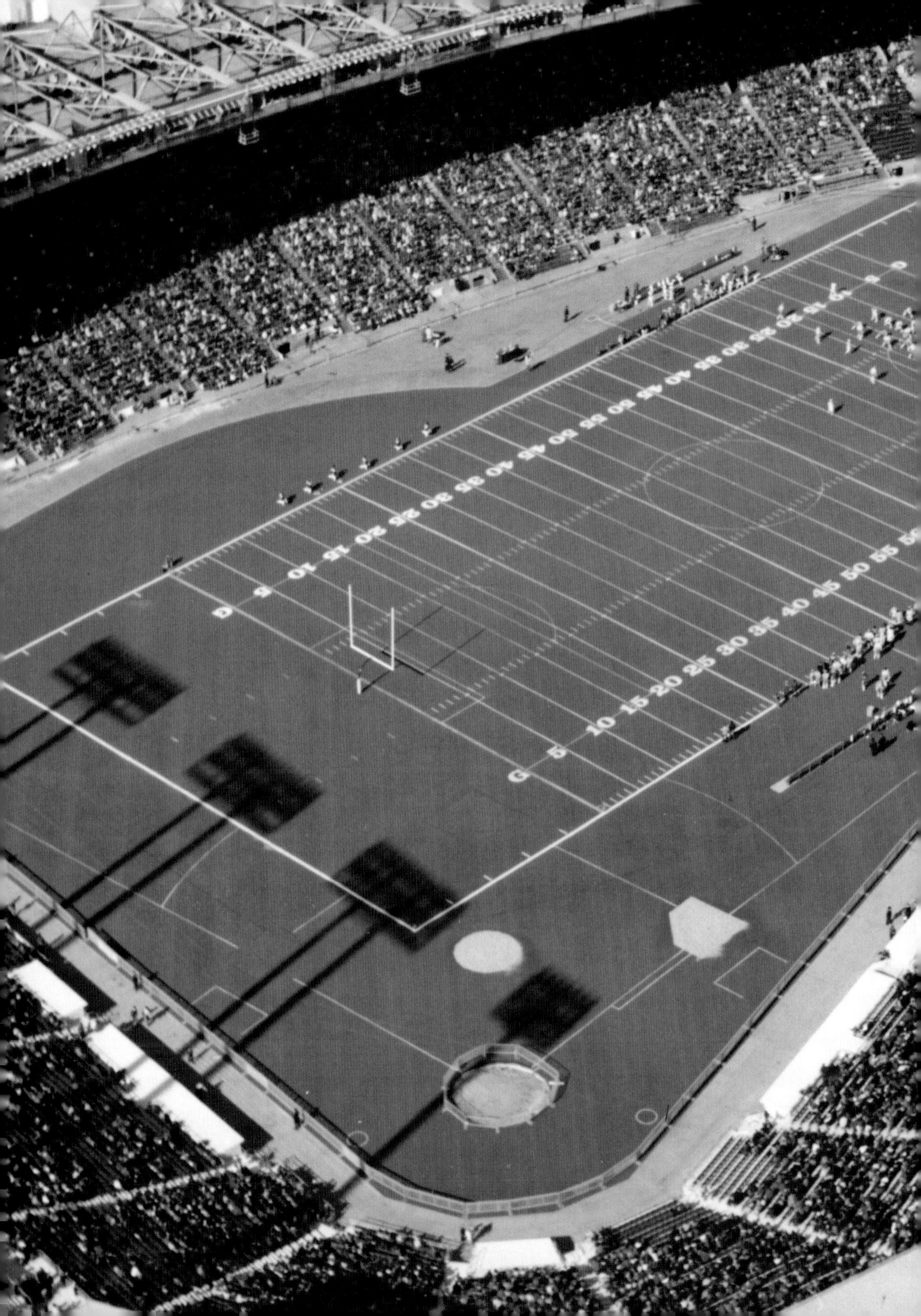

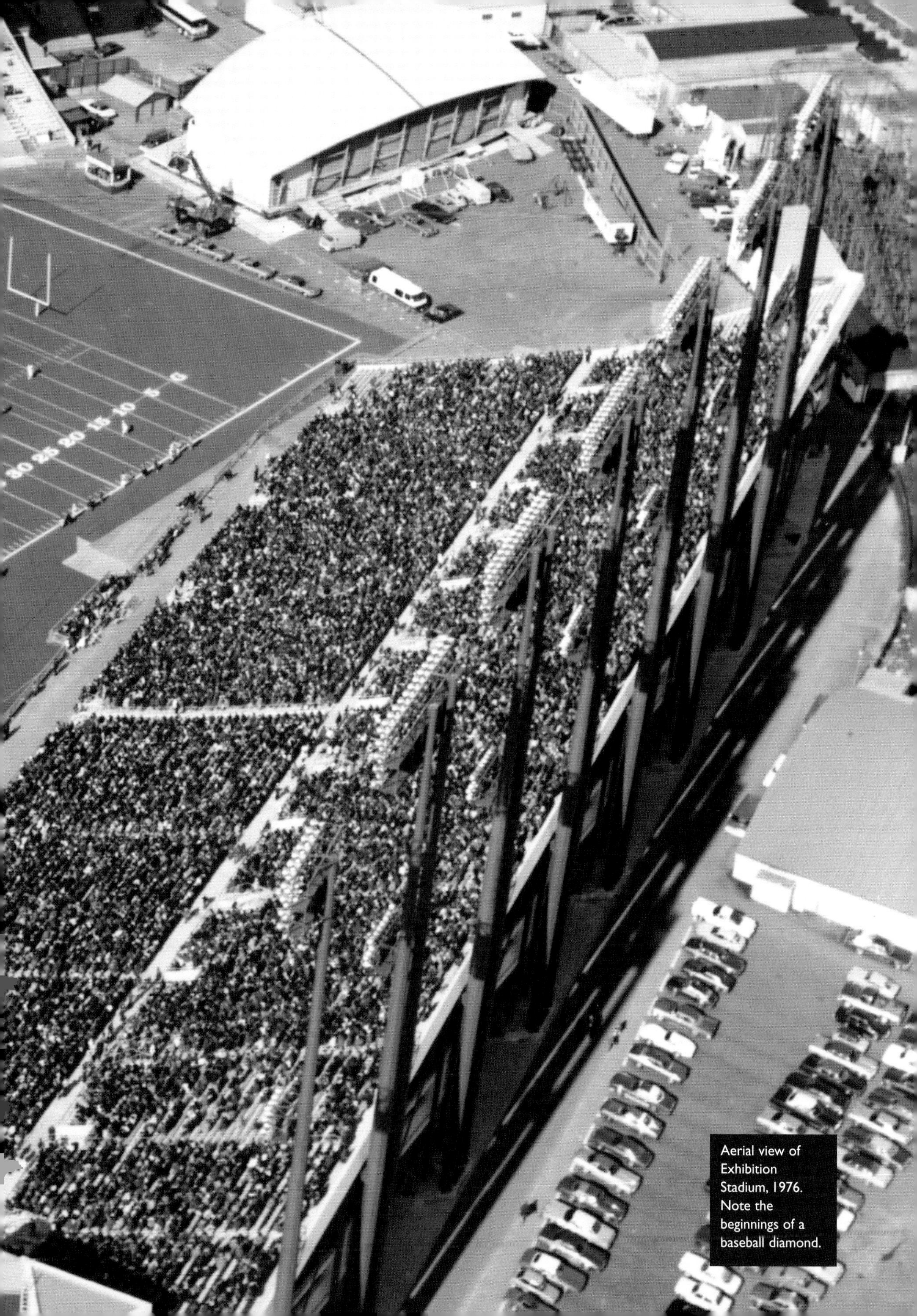

Aerial view of Exhibition Stadium, 1976. Note the beginnings of a baseball diamond.

One of his first moves in 1977 was to sign Harris, who was expected to be a first-round NFL draft pick, and insert him into a defence that featured the likes of Corrigall, rookie Paul Bennett, Lorne Richardson and Jim Marshall. After a slow start Cahill pushed the team to a third-place finish and their first playoff appearance in four years.

But it was a case of déjà vu for Cahill and the Argos in the East semi-final against Ottawa. With time running out, the Argos, trailing 21-16, had advanced to the Rough Riders' four-yard line. It seemed just a matter of a simple play would put the Argos into the end zone and onward to the division final. Cahill, figuring Ottawa would be expecting a running play, called for a pass. However, Rider defensive end Mike Fanucci, left unblocked, slammed into quarterback Chuck Ealey just as he was about to release the pass and the ball came loose. Fanucci also made the recovery.

It was 1971 all over again.

Cahill and the Argos would not recover from that setback. Even though they brought in NFL star Terry Metcalf in 1978 they would end up missing the playoffs for the fourth time in five years. After a 3-1 start, they went into a tailspin losing eight consecutive games and Hodgson fired Cahill. Assistant Bud Riley finished out the season.

Hodgson had also had enough. Before the next season he sold the club to Carling O'Keefe Brewery. Seeking to retain a high profile for the team, the brewery, through president Lew Hayman, brought in retired NFL star Forrest Gregg as head coach. Gregg, the Hall of Fame offensive lineman of the Green Bay Packers, then hired another NFL star, Willie Wood, as one of his assistants.

Gregg would last only a year with the Double Blue. After having difficulty adjusting to the Canadian game and compiling an unimpressive 5-11 season, Gregg jumped at an opportunity to return to the NFL as head coach of the Cincinnati Bengals. He turned the team over to Wood, who in 1980 became the CFL's first black head coach.

The Argos muddled through a 6-10 season under Wood in 1980, but with the acquisition of Holloway, running back Cedric Minter and the

FAN MEMORY

OFFSIDE OFFICIATING
BY CHRIS COMMINS

It was a pre-season battle at the CNE, Argos and Tiger-Cats, a really hot day. A very sloppy game, with dozens of penalties. Everyone was losing interest as the contest wound to a close. Argo ball near midfield, first and ten. Hamilton jumps offside, whistle goes, penalty marched off, first and five. Hamilton jumps offside again, the penalty is marched off, but the sticks don't move.

The Hamilton defensive captain looks over to the sideline, and asks for a measurement. The sticks come out, and the Argos are (apparently) about three inches short. "First down and inches" signals the head ref.

Nothing happens for a few moments, but finally, a second official runs over and speaks to the ref. He then signals the stickmen to move, indicates "first and ten," and the tedious game eventually finishes, to everyone's relief.

The only time in CFL history where two offsides didn't result in "first and ten!"

Above President Ralph Sazio and long-time club executive Lew Hayman.

Left Joe Barnes hands off to running back Cedric Minter, 1983.

Below Jan Carinci holds for Hank Ilesic, 1984.

ARGO MEMORY

BOB O'BILLOVICH

One of my most memorable experiences occurred in the 1983 Grey Cup win over B.C. We won the game 18-17. However, Hank Ilesic made the game closer than it should have been by missing three field goals.

After missing his third straight, I approached Hank and I reminded him that it was a very tight game and we were going to need every point we could get! He immediately responded by saying, "Don't worry coach, I'll make them when it counts!"

Hank lived up to his word when he made a 44-yarder in the fourth quarter to put us into position to win the game. We scored a late touchdown in the fourth quarter to take the lead 18-17. We failed on a two-point conversion attempt and the game ended 18-17.

I should mention that Ilesic's punting in that game, especially in the second half, largely contributed to our victory. So Hank played a big role in providing the fans with a very exciting game and I lost a few more hairs that day!

TOM TRIFAUX (50) AND THE O-LINE BLOCK FOR MARK JACKSON, 1980

JAN CARINCI RUNS INTERFERENCE FOR GEOFF TOWNSEND, 1984

presence of second-year receiver Terry Greer, the Argos appeared headed for brighter days. It was not to be. The losses piled up until they reached 10 without a win. Wood was canned and general manager Tommy Hudspeth took over for the rest of the year. However, the Argos managed just two wins over the final six games.

The Argos had not had a winning record in eight seasons and had finished dead last in the East in seven of those years. It was obvious to Carling O'Keefe that wholesale changes were needed.

In a shocking move, the beer boys took a brazen trip down the QEW to the lair of their arch-rivals, the hated Hamilton Tiger-Cats. There they talked the gruff, strong-minded Ralph Sazio, who as a player, coach, general manager and part-owner of the Tiger-Cats, was linked to Hamilton as much as the smoke-belching steel mills, and talked him into succeeding Hayman as the team's president.

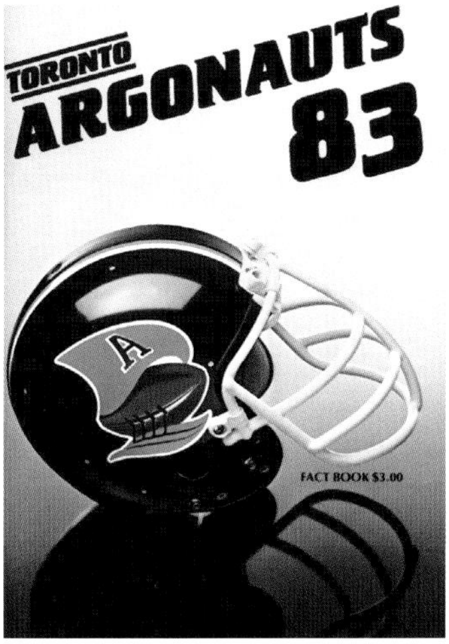

It was a move that was to turn the Argos almost instantly from perennial losers to champions.

Sazio went to Ottawa and hired O'Billovich, who was an assistant coach with the Rough Riders, as his field boss.

"One of the problems they had was hiring guys from the NFL who didn't know the Canadian game," said O'Billovich. "All they did was set the process back.

"But then they hired Ralph Sazio, who knew he had to find someone who knew the league. You have to understand the Canadian/American arrangement. He interviewed me and I guess he liked what I had to say. He hired me."

O'Billovich in turn brought in Darrell (Mouse) Davis as his offensive co-ordinator, who unveiled the run-and-shoot offence which was ideally suited to the quarterbacking talents of Holloway, whom the Argos had obtained from Ottawa a year earlier.

With that combination, the Boatmen made a dramatic turnaround going from the dismal 2-14 team of Wood and Hudspeth to Grey Cup finalists. While they managed a modest 9-6-1 record in the regular season, the Argos beat Ottawa in the division final and found themselves in the Grey Cup game for the first time in 12 years. Holloway was named

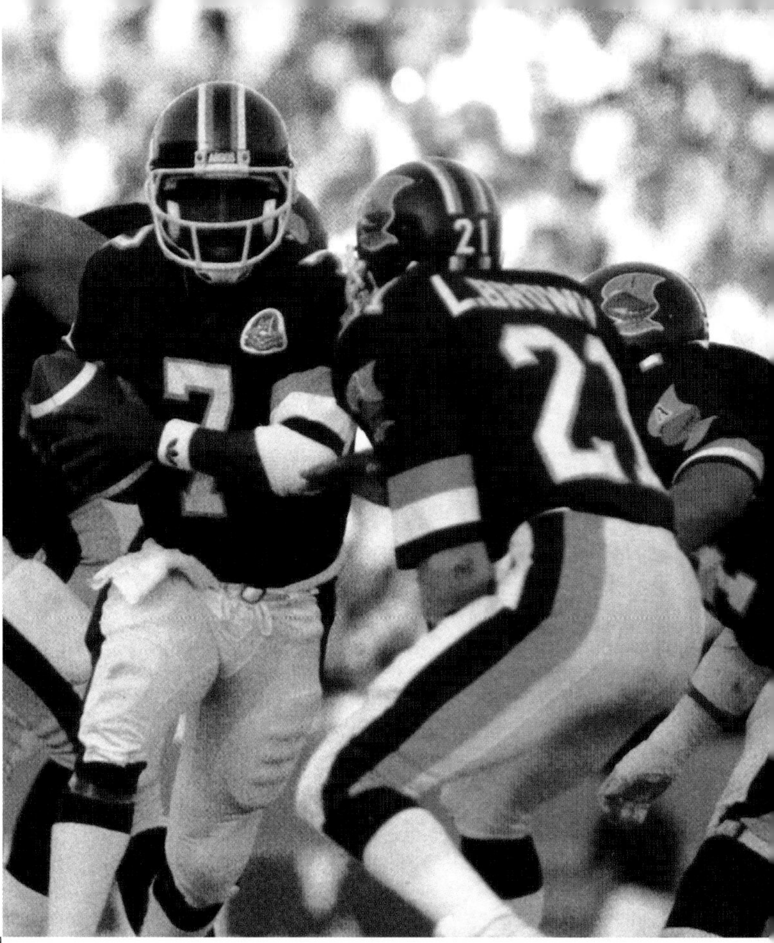

FAN MEMORY

THE BLOCKS
BY GLENN GRACIE

I have two memories.

The first is Condredge Holloway, date unknown, but against Ottawa he called a reverse. As the play came back across the pocket, Condredge threw a cross-body block that left both players prone on the field for some time. It was the most devastating block I have ever seen thrown by a quarterback.

The second is Mike Clemons, again against Ottawa, in 1996. Toronto was losing badly and Clemons, playing on special teams, made a sideline tackle to stop the Ottawa player. He came from nowhere and drove him—I believe the Ottawa player was Remy Trudel—out of bounds with unbelievable force.

These were the two most bone-crushing hits I can remember and I have enjoyed the Argos for 40 years.

FAN MEMORY

WHEN YOU GOTTA GO ...
BY MARK PANZER

Our family has been Argonaut supporters and season ticket holders since 1945, and my brother and I have owned the subscription since 1967. But our favourite family memory, or perhaps our most 'infamous' memory, comes from the early '80s.

I had begun taking my son Lenny, five or six years old at the time, to games. One day against Calgary at the CNE, the Argos were mounting a surprising and thrilling comeback in the dying seconds. Needing a touchdown to win, they were on the Stampeders five- or six-yard line with a few seconds to go.

The crowd was on its feet, the noise was deafening, the tension electric as the offence came over the ball. As we stood with our hearts in our throats waiting for the snap, my little guy looked up with a look of urgency. "Daddy, I have to go to the bathroom! REALLY BADLY!"

What was a staunch Argo fan to do? I grabbed an empty, large soft drink cup, and the situation was "relieved."

The Argos scored, the crowd went wild and we all went home happy. My brother Danny is still quick to retell this story (to my great embarrassment) whenever the family gets together and football is the subject of conversation.

(Lenny, now 30, remains an avid Argo fan and has given permission to tell this story.)

the CFL's outstanding player, only the second Argo to be accorded that honour.

The Argos, however, were no match for the powerful Edmonton Eskimos, who had won four consecutive championships. The Argos were to become the fifth and final victims of that powerful Edmonton dynasty losing 32-16 in a cold drizzle that marked the final Grey Cup game to be played at decaying Exhibition Stadium.

The Argos made up for that disappointment a year later in B.C. Place Stadium when their 18-17 win over the hometown Lions sent their own fans, 5,000 kilometres to the east in Toronto, spilling out onto Yonge St. in wild celebration. Thirty-one years of witnessing every one of the league's other eight cities enjoying a Grey Cup victory was finally over. Toronto partied long into the night.

"The team that was 2-14 in '81, reached the Grey Cup game the next year and then won it in '83," said Holloway. "The friendship and the

Left Condredge Holloway looking for Lester Brown, 1985.

Below Holloway hurdles for six, 1985.

Above Gil "The Thrill" Fenerty scrambles for yards against the B.C. Lions, 1988.

accomplishment of that group of guys will always be special to me."

Among the highlights of that season was the brilliant performance of Greer, who became the first CFL receiver to catch passes for more than 2,000 yards. It would be 11 more years before that mark would be broken by Calgary's Allen Pitts.

Greer, who eventually won a Super Bowl ring with the San Francisco 49ers, had 11 games in which he had more than 100 receiving yards, including eight in a row. He also had a game in which he caught 16 passes, a record he still shares today with two others.

The Sazio-O'Billovich era would last for another six years during which time the Argos would make one more trip to the Grey Cup game. That came in 1987 when they lost a 38-36 heartbreaker to—who else?—the Eskimos.

With Holloway being released after the '86 season, the Argos went with a trio of quarterbacks—Gilbert Renfroe, Danny Barrett and John Congemi—who, along with running back Gil (The Thrill) Fenerty, took the Argos to yet another battle with the Eskimos for Earl Grey's chalice.

A second championship of the decade appeared in the offing as Barrett scored on a 25-yard quarterback draw to put the Double Blue ahead 36-35 with less than 2:30 remaining. But the Eskimos battled back and, with 45 ticks left on the clock, Jerry Kauric booted a 49-yard field goal for the victory.

Time also began to tick down on the successful Sazio-O'Billovich run after that. The 1988 season saw Argos post a most impressive 12-4 record, the best won-loss mark in the team's history to that point. But Carling O'Keefe decided it was in the business of brewing beer not running a football team. Shortly after a 27-11 loss to the Winnipeg Blue Bombers in the East final had prevented them from making a second straight trip to the Grey Cup game, the brewery sold the team to Toronto-born entrepreneur Harry Ornest, who by then was making his home in Los Angeles.

Darrell K. Smith, 1986-92.

The Argos inexplicably struggled the following season under their new owner, and the frugal Ornest began to complain he was losing as much as $180,000 a game as the crowds flattened out in the mid-30,000 range rather than the 50,000 or more he had expected. The season concluded with only the second losing record of the previous eight years and Ornest, as owners are wont to do, fired his coach.

Canadian linebacker Don Moen arrived with the Argos at the same time as O'Billovich and enjoyed the high points of the era. But he was also around for the decline.

"In 1982, football was king in Toronto," he said. "People were starved for it. They knew who you were. People were passionate about the Argos. In 1983 we won the Cup. I sometimes wonder if that was the worst thing that happened. What do people grab for after that?"

Moen, now a successful vice-president of marketing for The Score sports television channel, recalled that the team failed to move forward with its marketing.

"It was little things like when the SkyDome opened people had to buy Jays tickets when you bought a sky box, but not Argos tickets. There had to be a change in the perception of the Argonauts and where they fit into the sports picture in Toronto. But the Argos didn't have the resources to

ARGO MEMORY

TERRY GREER

After being part of two dismal seasons, 1980 and 1981, nothing can top the feeling of going to the Grey Cup in 1983. My most memorable moment occured in 1983, the final game of the regular season.

I knew I was approaching an all-time record for reception yards in one season. Joe Barnes informed me in the huddle that I needed about eight yards to reach 2,000 yards. When the huddle broke, I noticed my teammates standing along the sideline watching in anticipation. Joe threw the ball, I caught it, gaining 13 yards, and went out of bounds. At that point I became the first receiver to gain 2,000 yards in one season. Then I noticed all my teamates charging towards me. They lifted me in the air in celebration.

I can't explain the feeling I had at that time. The way they embraced my 2,003 yard record showed the character and camaraderie of that1983 Grey Cup championship team.

Right General Manager Mike McCarthy and Terry Greer during a halftime ceremony honouring Darrell K. Smith, who passed Greer to become the Argos' all-time leading receiver, 1992.

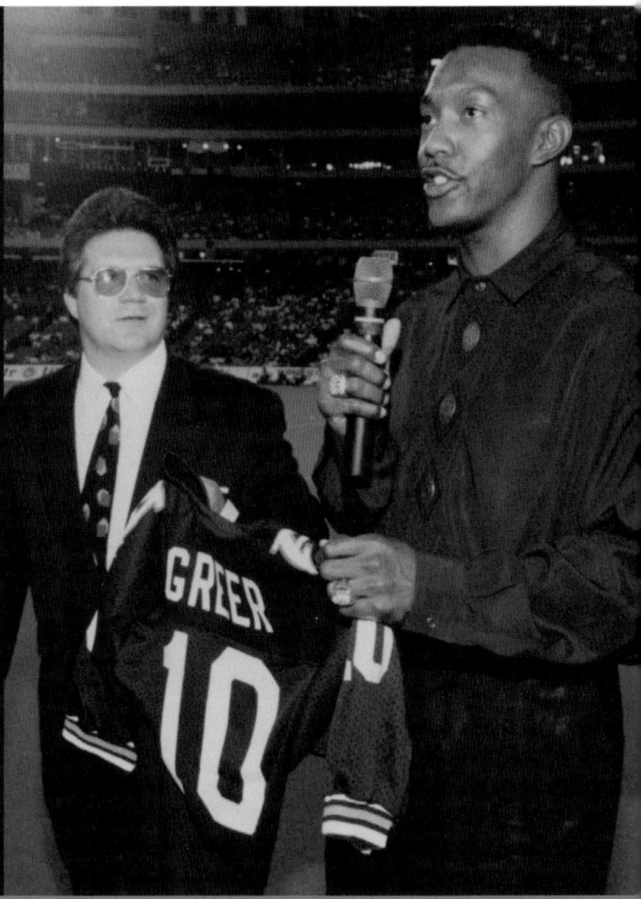

REGGIE PLEASANT, 1987-94

DON MOEN, 1982-94

do that. We had good players, good talent and the SkyDome. We'd get 25,000 people in there and that would have been good every place else, but in the SkyDome it looked half full."

Another star of that era, guard Dan Ferrone, said he now looks back at those times with a different view than when he was on the rollercoaster ride.

"My first year was the worst season in team history," he said. "But now I look back and say it was nothing but fun. Playing for the Argos all those years shaped my life: how I act today, how I work, how I interact with people. All those things."

O'Billovich's final year as Argo coach, however, was not without a significant moment.

Fenerty, who thrilled the fans for three seasons, set an Argo single-season rushing mark when he ran for 1,247 yards despite missing two games with a pulled hamstring muscle. However, it would be his final year as an Argo.

He was unhappy with the Argo offence employed by O'Billovich and had played out his option. The following spring he signed with the NFL Saints, in his hometown of New Orleans.

"There wasn't enough money in the organization to keep me," he explained after signing with the Saints. "I wasn't happy with the way things were going offensively. They didn't have an offensive co-ordinator and the defences around the league knew all our plays before we even ran them."

The Argos, however, had a replacement waiting in the wings. Mike Clemons, a 5-foot-5 running back from Dunedin, Florida, had joined the Argos that year and, while he saw limited action as a ball carrier because of Fenerty's presence, he showed promise of things to come.

It was Obie who inadvertently gave the elusive scatback the nickname by which he would become as well—if not better—known than his given name.

As he watched the pint-sized ball carrier zig-zag through the defence, bouncing off would-be tacklers during training camp, O'Billovich exclaimed: "Ding-dang, that little guy bounces around out there like a pinball."

It stuck. Pinball Clemons was born.

~ RICK MATSUMOTO

Images
1973–1990

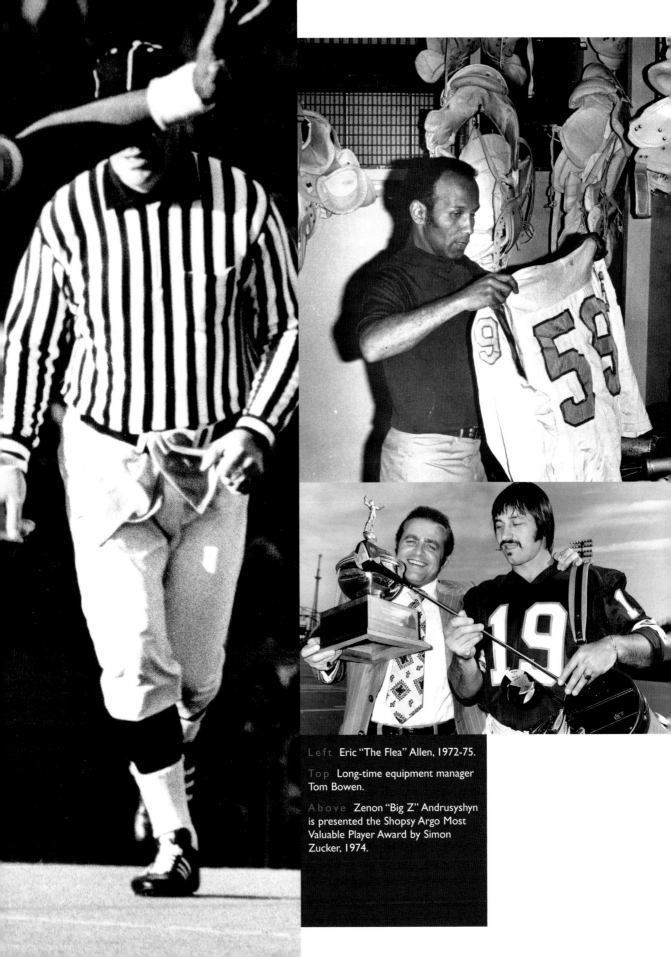

Left Eric "The Flea" Allen, 1972-75.

Top Long-time equipment manager Tom Bowen.

Above Zenon "Big Z" Andrusyshyn is presented the Shopsy Argo Most Valuable Player Award by Simon Zucker, 1974.

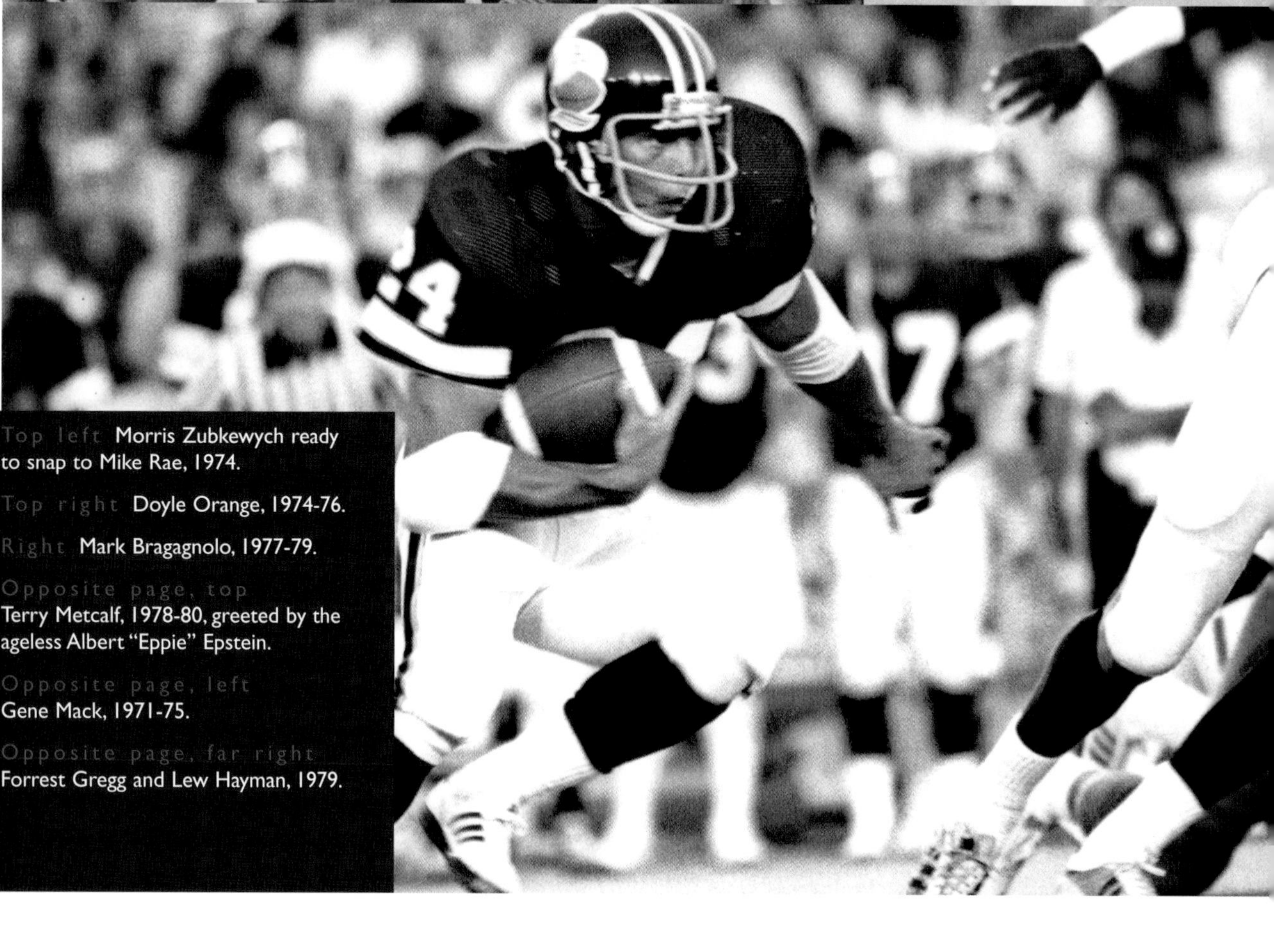

Top left Morris Zubkewych ready to snap to Mike Rae, 1974.

Top right Doyle Orange, 1974-76.

Right Mark Bragagnolo, 1977-79.

Opposite page, top
Terry Metcalf, 1978-80, greeted by the ageless Albert "Eppie" Epstein.

Opposite page, left
Gene Mack, 1971-75.

Opposite page, far right
Forrest Gregg and Lew Hayman, 1979.

ARGOS

Argo quarterback Chuck Ealey, throws over an Ottawa Rough Rider defender, 1976.

77

HE BLUES NEXT GAME
ARGOS
22
21

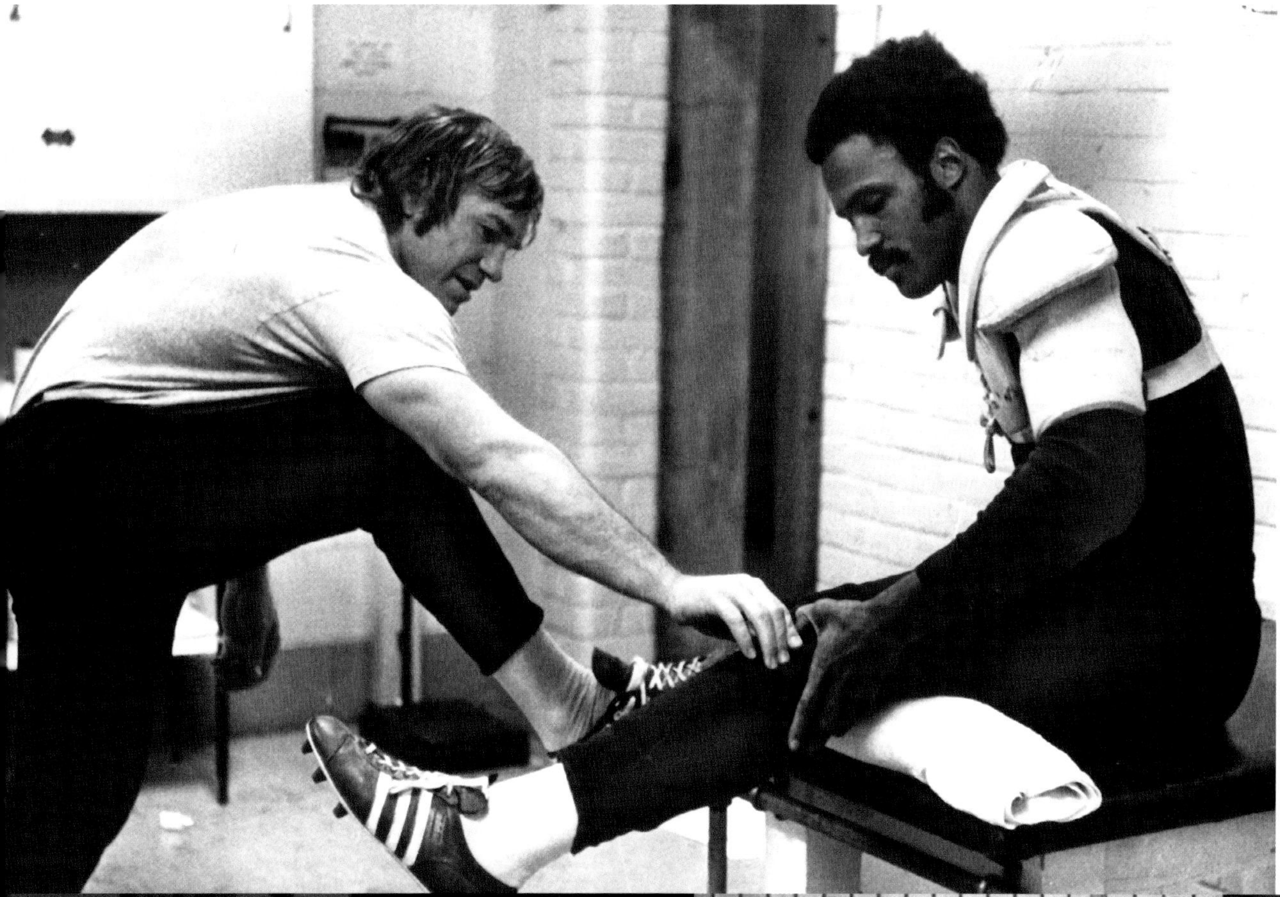

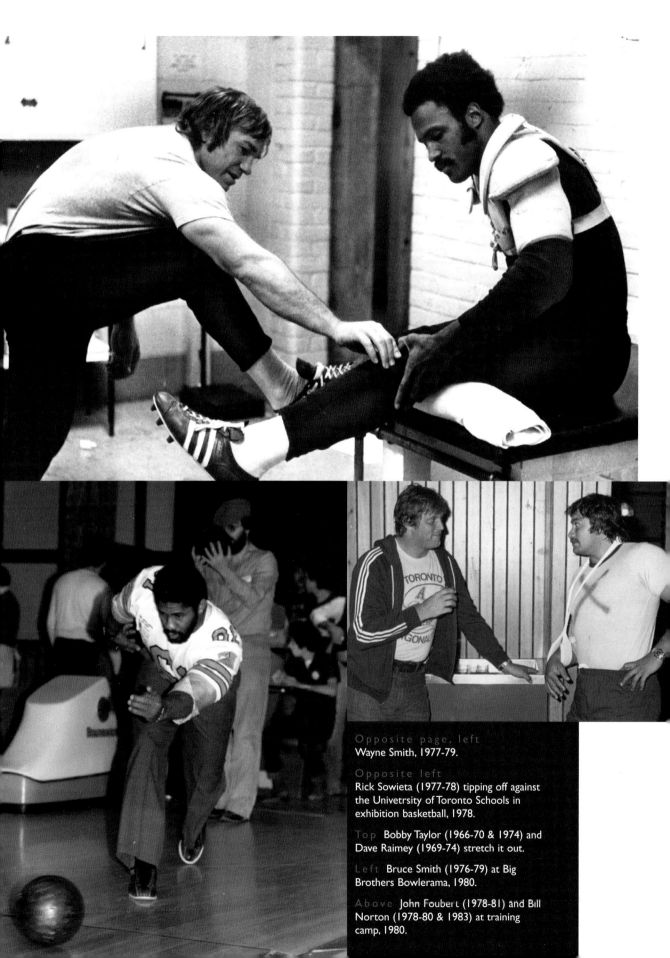

Opposite page, left
Wayne Smith, 1977-79.

Opposite left
Rick Sowieta (1977-78) tipping off against the Univetrsity of Toronto Schools in exhibition basketball, 1978.

Top Bobby Taylor (1966-70 & 1974) and Dave Raimey (1969-74) stretch it out.

Left Bruce Smith (1976-79) at Big Brothers Bowlerama, 1980.

Above John Foubert (1978-81) and Bill Norton (1978-80 & 1983) at training camp, 1980.

Left New head coach Willie Wood is introduced by Lew Hayman, 1980.

Below Terry Metcalf, 1978-80.

Right Lance Chomyc, 1985-93.

Far right Jan Carinci, 1981-88.

Below right Paul Pearson, 1979-87.

pizza

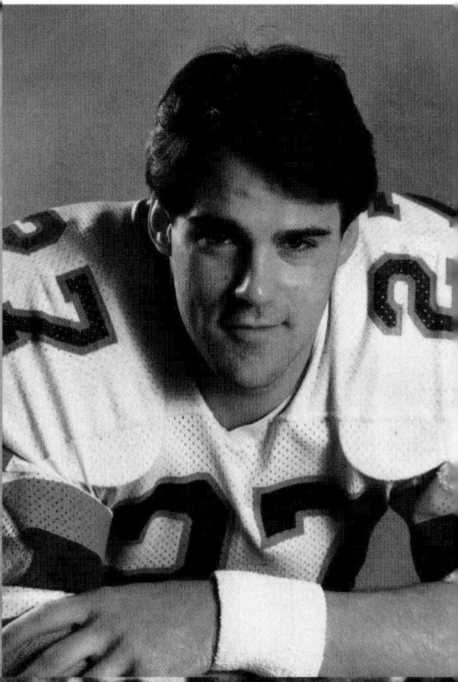

Jim Corrigall performs a celebratory cartwheel after a sack.

This page Carl Brazley (2), Joe Barnes (17) and head coach Bob O'Billovich celebrate the end of the Grey Cup drought, 1983.

Opposite, top left
Bob Bronk and Joe Barnes on the move, 1983.

Opposite, top right
Cedric Minter, 1981-83 & 1986.

Opposite, below
Terry Greer, 1981-85.

34
17

10

IAN BECKSTEAD AND CHRIS SCHULTZ HELP OUT DANNY BARRETT, 1987

GLENN KULKA AND WILLIE PLESS GET IT DONE AGAINST THE TICATS, 1988

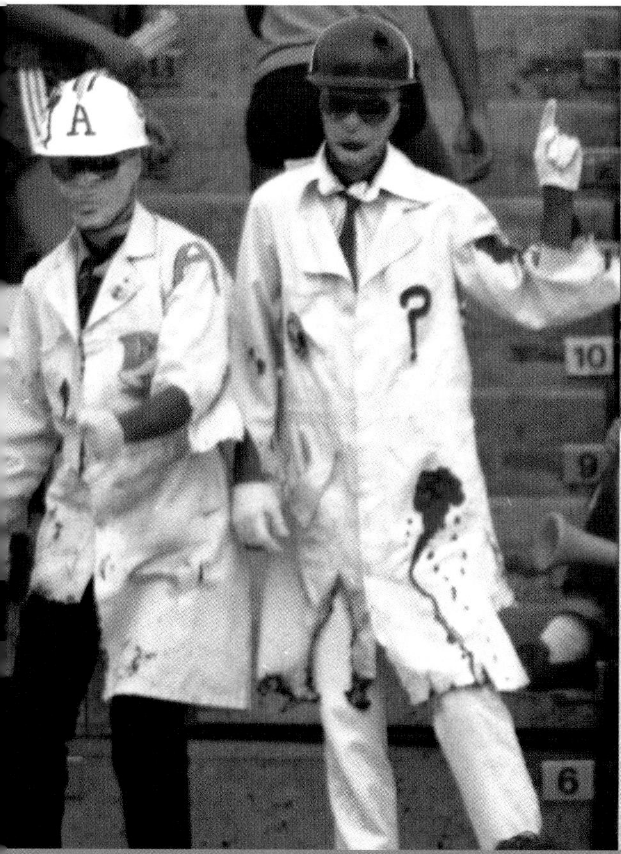

HANGING OUT AT EXHIBITION PLACE

A NEW HOME AT SKYDOME

Right Glenn Kulka (1987-89) and Bruce Holmes (1988-89 & 1992).

Below Darrell K. Smith.

Below right Rodney Harding, 1985-94.

Opposite page Danny Barrett, 1985 & 1987-88.

canadian
31

SECTION 6

6

1991-2003

Boom and Bust

As anyone who has stood over a pinball machine in an arcade knows, you play one ball at a time. But in 1990, the Argonauts found that with Mike Clemons, dubbed Pinball by head coach Bob O'Billovich, it was like playing four balls at one time.

Clemons was an all-purpose workhorse. Rushing, catching passes, returning punts and returning kickoffs, the diminutive Clemons set a CFL record for all-purpose yardage (3,840) in a single season that still stands today. That feat earned him the CFL's outstanding player award, and made him the third Argo—joining Bill Symons (1968) and Condredge Holloway (1982)—to achieve that honour.

However, when Clemons arrived at training camp six months later for the 1991 season, he found himself sharing the marquee with a rookie wide receiver and glamorous new owners. The wide receiver, out of the University of Notre Dame, was Raghib Ismail, who had his own nickname—Rocket. The owners comprised the Hollywood trio of Wayne Gretzky, John Candy and Bruce McNall.

Left Wayne Gretzky hoists his first Grey Cup after four Stanley Cups.

Previous page Michael "Pinball" Clemons, 1989-2000.

The new owners arrived despite the revival of the team's fortunes a year earlier under coach Don Matthews and owner Harry Ornest. When the frugal Ornest became involved in a boardroom battle at Hollywood Park race track near his Los Angeles home, he decided to focus on acquiring a majority share of the racetrack and hung the "for sale" sign on the Argonauts.

McNall, who owned the NHL's Los Angeles Kings hockey club, was also on the board of Hollywood Park. When Ornest let it be known his CFL team was on the market, McNall was intrigued. The multi-

ARGO MEMORY

DANNY WEBB, EQUIPMENT MANAGER

Candy and I hit it off from the start. There were many times I would get a call at work. It would be John from L.A. just keeping tabs on how the guys were preparing for that week's game and seeking an update on injuries. John hated to miss games and would charter Lee Iacoccaa's jet to get to our home and away games. He would keep guys loose before games with his humour, and cheer them on from the sidelines during the game.

During pre-game warm-ups, it would be just him and me in the dressing room. You could tell it was a big game as John would chain smoke as he helped me hand out towels and gave me his game plan. During the game he would hand out water, and help me carry off injured players as well as be our biggest cheerleader. He wanted the Argos to be the class of the CFL, whether it was decks of cards with the Argo logo on it or a cappuccino and espresso machine in the dressing room just in case Dan Ferrone wanted a cup.

In fitting fashion we won the Grey Cup in 1991. To see John crying like a kid solidified our belief that he genuinely cared for the Argonauts and the CFL.

Above The larger-than-life John Candy, with Argo Kelvin Pruenster (1983-92) and Kelvin's son.

Opposite, bottom John's mother Evangeline, with John's brother, Jim, surrounded by Argos Don Moen, Reggie Pleasant, Pierre Vercheval and Michael Clemons.

ARGO MEMORY

DON MOEN

Nineteen-ninety-one was an incredible year: the ownership of Gretzky, Candy, McNall; the signing of Rocket Ismail; the quarterbacking/leadership of Matt Dunigan. The entire season, on and off the field, was unforgettable. Our record was great, everywhere we played the crowds were big, and there were always Hollywood celebrities around.

Personally, I had one of my best seasons. The East final, where I was defensive player of the game, and the Grey Cup were probably my two best games that year. John Candy was with us at every home and away game. John was probably the most genuine, passionate person I ever met.

After we won the Grey Cup, Dan Ferrone and I were presented the trophy, and I ran with it down the tunnel into our dressing room where everyone was going crazy. Standing beside my locker was John, tears streaming down his cheeks. He had put his heart and soul into that team and his emotions were streaming out. My biggest memory—and the culmination of the year—was embracing John in a "guy" hug and sharing tears of joy, and, later with my wife, having a post-game dinner celebration with John. Unforgettable.

ARGO MEMORY

MATT DUNIGAN

Although I played only two seasons and 17 1/2 games in an Argo uniform, I had some awesome times. My running mates were Andrew Murray, Paul Masotti, Blaine Schmidt, Mike Campbell, David Williams, Rodney Harding, Chris Schultz, D.K. Smith and Paul Nastasiuk, just to name a few. But one memory stands out.

The Candy Man Experience: Toronto at Calgary, 1991. Rocket Ismail and I had both sustained significant injuries in a hard-fought contest. Rocket suffered a serious concussion and I broke my collarbone. After the game, I remember going to the hospital with John Candy, Sue Waks, Wayne Gretzky and Bruce McNall to see how, Raghib, the "franchise," was doing. That alone should give you insight into the quality of the caring people we had running the organization.

After visiting with Rocket, John offered to take me back to the hotel for some food and beverage. Now, that's an offer you don't get every day! I thought about it for a nano-second and said, "I'm in!"

Up to his sweet suite we went and when I walked in the door, there was this spread of food laid out that could have fed the entire team. So I commenced eating as best I could with one hand while John tended to the beverages. Returning with our beverages, John asked if I needed something else for my pain. I inquisitively looked up and inquired, "What do you have?"

John dashed out of the room and came back with enough pain medications to make a drug store envious! Needless to say, my pain was soon under control and John and I had the chance to relax and share another great time.

I don't remember the flight back to Toronto!

Hollywood came north, complete with glitz and glamour on and off the field

millionaire entrepreneur, who dabbled in, among other things, coin collecting, huddled with his superstar, Gretzky, and popular Toronto-born actor/comedian Candy and the trio purchased the Argos in the spring of 1991.

Hollywood came north, complete with glitz and glamour on and off the field. The new owners held a gala, coming-out party at the Horseshoe Tavern that was highlighted by a performance of the Blues Brothers routine starring Dan Ackroyd and Candy. The presence of No. 99, who made hockey fashionable in Los Angeles after McNall bought his contract from the Edmonton Oilers for $16 million, and the enthusiastic Candy, who grew up in East York as an Argo fan while playing football at Neil McNeil High School, attracted immediate attention from fans not only in Toronto, but across the league. But there was more.

The Rocket.

Ismail was the biggest name in U.S. college football at the time. The speedy receiver was widely expected to be the No. 1 pick in that spring's NFL draft. However, the Argos stepped in with a four-year, $18-million offer that included incentives based on attendance that could raise his earnings to $26 million. Ismail decided the NFL could wait.

A confident 21-year-old, Ismail was not intimidated by the pressure to produce on the field to earn his huge salary, nor of having to sell Torontonians on the Argos, a money-losing venture for previous owners.

"I've been dealing with pressure all through my career," he told the *Toronto Star*. "When you're dealing with a place like Notre Dame, you learn what pressure is all about. At Notre Dame people aren't just satisfied if you win. If you win but didn't play a good game they're still not satisfied."

1990s

He promised not to disappoint Argo fans.

"If they come to see me play I'll try my best to please them," he vowed. The Rocket did please fans, but more so in other CFL cities than in Toronto. The Argos played to near-capacity crowds in Vancouver, Regina and Edmonton. But at the SkyDome the Argos managed an average of just slightly more than 36,500 fans. While that was 14,000

Left and above Raghib "Rocket" Ismail at his introductory press conference and on the run, 1991.

Below Kevin Smellie eluding tacklers, 1992.

MATT DUNIGAN MARSHALS THE TROOPS DURING THE 1991 GREY CUP GAME

J.P. IZQUIERDO ELUDES THE BLUE BOMBERS, 1996

BRUCE ELLIOTT LOOKS FOR SOMEONE TO BLOCK

DAN FERRONE AND OFFENSIVE LINE MATES, 1991

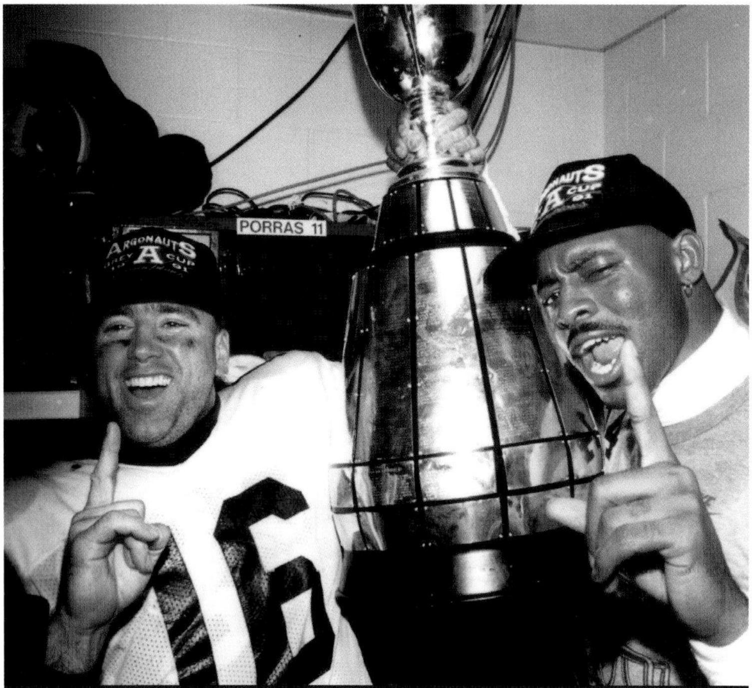

ARGO MEMORY

ADAM RITA

I'll never forget a conversation I had with backup quarterback Rickey Foggie the night before the 1991 Grey Cup game against the Calgary Stampeders in the freezing cold of Winnipeg.

I was the coach at the time and had basically decided (No. 1 quarterback) Matt Dunigan was not going to play. But then (general manager) Mike McCarthy came up to me and says: "Dunigan is thinking of playing." Well he hadn't practiced all week. He had a broken collarbone.

I said, "If he's going to play I need clearance from the doctor, his wife, his parents, and then you're going to have to convince me it's not going to be a career-ending type of injury if he takes another hit." I got all that.

The thing about Matty was that he had never won a Grey Cup game as the starting quarterback. So I really wanted him to win one. But not at the expense of his career.

After he worked out that Saturday (secretly, in the hotel ballroom) I had to go to Rickey Foggie (who was slated to be the starting quarterback). I'll never forget the conversation I had with Rickey.

After I told him everything, he looked at me and said: "Coach, if I was the starting quarterback and I had a broken collarbone and came to you and asked you to let me play in the Grey Cup game, would you do that for me?"

I replied: "Yes, I would."

He said: "Then Matty should start."

That to me was very heart-warming. He could have pouted and done a lot of things. Instead he took the high road. I'll never forget that.

FAN MEMORY

BY KEITH QUIGG

I've been an Argo fan all my life and a season ticket holder for a long time. My wife arranged to have a surprise 50th birthday party for me at the SkyDome during an Argos game. She booked a field-view room for the night, and, unknown to me, invited lots of friends to visit with us.

After a friend and I left the room and got to our seats (Sect. 112) to watch the game, I looked up beside the JumboTron and saw a 10-x-14 foot banner hanging out of our hotel room window that said "Happy 50th Birthday Keith" (I still have the banner).

I love my wife dearly (we've been married for almost 30 years); however, I only turned 49 that weekend. I'm 54 now and my wife Carol still thinks I'm a year older.

I was so appreciative of her gesture that, to this day, I have never said a thing.

Left Matt Dunigan and Rickey Foggie.

Right Dan Ferrone, 1981-88, 1990-92.

FAN MEMORY

BY MIKE HAMMOND

The Immaculate Reception: 1991, Section 28, Ivor Wynne Stadium ... Foggie to Hammond ... complete!

Cheering for the Double Blue in my home town of Hamilton has never been easy, but it's a challenge I've embraced for 30 years.

For the game in question, I was joined by four buddies (all Ticat fans), who settled in with me to watch the heated rivalry. During the second half, Foggie scored a TD in the west end zone, bringing me to my feet and rendering my pals silent. Rickey then looked up into the stands, acknowledged my celebration and unleashed a perfect pass to me. The completion never entered the official stats but it will be forever remembered by five guys from Steeltown.

Some years later when Rickey became the Ticats QB, I relayed the story to him and had him sign the ball. That pigskin treasure is displayed proudly in my rec room and a great Argos memory is enshrined in my mind.

more per game than the team averaged in their final season at Exhibition Stadium, it was far below the 53,000 or so that McNall had envisioned.

Still, at season's end, the investment in Ismail paid off in the most important way—winning the Grey Cup. The Rocket played a huge role in that victory, contributing an electrifying 87-yard touchdown sprint in the fourth quarter to lift the Argos to a 36-21 triumph over the Calgary Stampeders at Winnipeg Stadium in the coldest championship game ever played. Temperatures had dropped to minus-17 Celsius as Ismail sped down the sideline and deftly avoided a frozen can of beer tossed by a (Stampeder?) fan.

The victory was also notable by the fact quarterback Matt Dunigan performed with a broken collarbone, medically numbed by the team doctor, after he had tested it the night before by throwing in a secret session in the ballroom of the team's hotel.

While 1991 began and ended in true Hollywood fashion, it turned into a horror show just nine months later. Despite the Grey Cup victory the

ARGO MEMORY

DAN FERRONE

A very memorable Argo moment happened for me at the 1991 Grey Cup game in Winnipeg—the coldest Grey Cup in history.

Owners Bruce McNall, John Candy and Wayne Gretzky's investment in The Rocket (Raghib Ismail) paid off that day with his thrilling kickoff return for a touchdown that clinched the championship for us.

As Argos co-captain it was my honour to be presented with the Grey Cup. Back at my locker, I was surprised to find Candy, Gretzky and his wife, Janet, neaby, hiding from the mob. It was a chaotic locker room, jam-packed with media, cameras, celebrities, players, coaches and league personnel.

In all the mayhem, I was shocked to see that my nine-year-old son, Matthew, had made his way into the locker room. His eyes had welled up and he had tears running down his cheeks. Wow! What a special moment.

We had just finished a Hollywood-story season. I was holding the legendary Grey Cup and I was able to share this incredible moment with my first child.

I stood up and opened my arms and called to my son. He suddenly motioned with his arm and said: "Dad, get out of the way ... that's Wayne Gretzky!"

Argos lost $3.5 million. The red ink had a direct effect on the 1992 season. To start with, the Argos were unwilling to give Dunigan, who had played out his option and missed most of the 1991 season due to injury, a new contract in the $450,000 to $500,000 range. He eventually jumped to the Winnipeg Blue Bombers as a free agent.

It isn't over until the extremely fat lady sings or the extremely fat man cuts you

The loss of Dunigan was probably the most profound factor in the team's struggle in '92. Rickey Foggie was handed the starting job backed up by newcomers John Congemi and Mike Kerrigan. But Foggie suffered a cracked bone in his ankle in a pre-season game and, while he continued to play, he was ineffective. By September, with the team sporting a 3-8 record, Adam Rita, who had been named coach of the year only months before, was fired and replaced by assistant Dennis Meyer.

"Matt was gone. That was the biggest thing," said Rita in reflecting how the team sagged so badly after the Grey Cup win. "And then, having Rickey injured was tough. We got a little complacent as a team. No matter what I did I couldn't get them out of the doldrums.

"We were never able to overcome our injuries. We didn't have the same kind of depth that we had the previous two years. The ownership wasn't spending money any more."

When the Argos missed the playoffs, ownership decided the Rocket had run out of fuel as far as his usefulness to the organization was concerned. While he did everything he was asked to do on the field, his off-field antics were beginning to wear thin. He would refuse to talk to the media or do public relations appearances, things that he was expected to do to help put fans in the stands to pay his huge salary. His exit was greased when he was quoted saying: "It isn't over until the extremely fat lady sings or the extremely fat man cuts you." Many people felt he was referring to the rotund McNall.

Rickey Foggie, 1990-92.

Before the start of the 1993 season, the Argos, Ismail and the Los Angeles Raiders, who had obtained his NFL rights, made a deal that propelled the Rocket out of Toronto. At the same time, the CFL began a short-lived expansion into the U.S. and the Argos' fortunes plummeted both on the field and at the box office. Meyer was replaced midway

ARGO MEMORY

PAUL MASOTTI

It was still snowing when the game began

I remember waking up in our Hamilton hotel the morning of the 1996 Grey Cup game and looking outside to check the weather. I felt pretty charged up that morning, anyway, but when I saw enormous snow flakes falling past the window it enhanced my excitement and kindled memories of my childhood.

This was the weather in which my brothers and I would play "make me dive" on the front lawn or in the back yard when we were kids in Stoney Creek. One of us would run across the lawn and the other would throw the football to an uncatchable spot. The idea was to make the receiver dive either over the bushes or into the freshly formed snowdrift to catch the ball.

It was still snowing when the game began. It was a beautiful night—not too cold, virtually no wind and the slowly falling snow created a peaceful, almost surreal atmosphere. You couldn't see the lines on the field and the footing was terrible, but the game was as exciting as any in which I ever played.

There were 80 points scored and we won, 43-37.

Each Grey Cup I played in had a special meaning for me. The 1991 game was my first. In the '97 game I was voted top Canadian and received a truck from Doug Flutie, who had won it as the game's top player but graciously turned the keys over to me.

But the '96 Cup, in my home town with all my family and friends in the crowd and all that snow, was easily my favourite moment as an Argonaut.

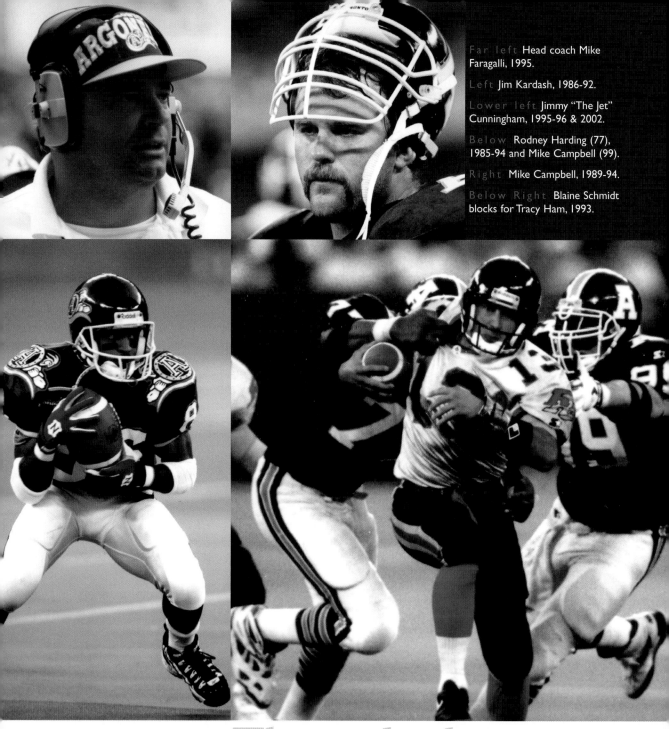

Far left Head coach Mike Faragalli, 1995.

Left Jim Kardash, 1986-92.

Lower left Jimmy "The Jet" Cunningham, 1995-96 & 2002.

Below Rodney Harding (77), 1985-94 and Mike Campbell (99).

Right Mike Campbell, 1989-94.

Below Right Blaine Schmidt blocks for Tracy Ham, 1993.

The only thing that was constant was change

99

A
54

FAN MEMORY

BY MATTHEW MCKENZIE

My first ever Grey Cup was in 1996 when a friend and I decided to make the three-hour drive to Hamilton to catch the Argos versus the Eskimos. It was a classic game, with snowy weather providing an ideal backdrop, but we sat in what I thought would be terrible seats in the temporary section right behind one of the field goal posts. However, our less than ideal seats resulted in me taking home the ultimate Grey Cup souvenir: a Grey Cup ball kicked by Mike Vanderjagt and held by Doug Flutie.

At some point during the game I had to answer the call of nature. So I ventured to one of Ivor Wynne's washrooms, ball in hand, where the mix of fans "doing their business" and the cold made for some steamy conditions Many noticed what I was carrying and asked to examine the ball. Without hesitation, I allowed the ball to pass around the room and, as it made the rounds, the room suddenly erupted in a chant of "CFL, CFL!"

It was because of this experience (and my surprise that I actually got the ball back) that I became an Argo and CFL fan for life.

Right Don Wilson and Ken Benson following the 1996 Grey Cup victory.

Below Pinball Clemons signs for fans.

FAN MEMORY

BY JULIA CHMILNITZKY

One summer day, when Pinball Clemons was still a player, I was at the Toronto International Airport to connect with my mother, who was on her way to Vancouver. But I somehow missed her.

While waiting near the entrance to the security area, and feeling despondent for failing to connect with my mom, I looked up and— "Oh my God"—there was my football hero, Pinball, and the rest of the players heading towards security on their way to Vancouver.

I can't believe what I did next. Here I was, a 50-something teacher, and I let out a scream— "PINBALL!"—as I ran toward him. I'll never forget how he turned, his arms out to embrace me. I was so sad that I didn't connect with my mom but Pinball's warmth and acceptance will live in my heart forever.

through the '93 season with the second coming of O'Billovich as head coach. Attendance at the SkyDome was rapidly sinking and the "for sale" sign went up again as the team continued to lose money.

"Quick," McNall was heard to quip prior to a game as he scanned the players clothes hanging in the Argos' empty dressing room. "Go through the pockets and see if there's any loose change. We might need it."

The sudden death of Candy, who was seeking the resources to buy out McNall and Gretzky, resulted in the club ultimately being sold to TSN the following spring. Two more years of futility would follow, however, until the owners cleaned house by firing O'Billovich and bringing back another re-tread in Don Matthews for the 1996 season, giving him the dual title of head coach and director of football operations.

Wide receiver Paul Masotti, who played 12 seasons with the Argos and retired after the 1999 season as the club's all-time pass reception yardage leader, remembers the rollercoaster ride through this period.

"I guess the only thing that was constant was change," said Masotti. "I don't think I played with the same quarterback for more than two years. It was feast or famine. We were either 3-15 or 15-3."

Matthews had helped write history the previous year by leading the Baltimore Stallions to a Grey Cup victory and making them the only non-Canadian-based team to win the CFL title. However, the CFL's ill-conceived expansion into the U.S. was coming to an end and the future of the Baltimore franchise was uncertain. It would end up in Montreal as the reincarnation of the Alouettes, but the nomadic Matthews was looking to make a change. And the Argos were willing to provide him with a new/old home.

One of Matthews' first moves as director of football operations was to sign free agent quarterback Doug Flutie, who had led the Calgary Stampeders to two Grey Cup appearances in four years (winning in '92). He became available when Stampeder owner Larry Ryckman declared bankruptcy. The acquisition of Flutie to go along with a star-studded lineup that included Clemons, Robert Drummond, Masotti and Mike O'Shea brought instant success on the field. The Argos finished first with

I'm not going to swallow swords at Square One and Doug Flutie's not going to walk on hot coals

a 15-3 record. But to the dismay of players, the front office and owners TSN Enterprises, fan support was well short of what was needed to pay Flutie a reported $1-million and Matthews, $300,000.

When the Argos clinched first place on October 6 with an impressive 28-14 win over the Winnipeg Blue Bombers, only 17,310 spectators were in the cavernous SkyDome where the roof was open to the glorious autumn afternoon.

"It's getting more and more discouraging all the time," tackle Vic Stevenson said at the time. "I don't know what more we can do, but play well and win. We're not circus performers. I'm not going to swallow swords at Square One (shopping mall) and Doug Flutie's not going to walk on hot coals."

But despite fan indifference, the Argos captured the Grey Cup on a snowy afternoon at Hamilton's Ivor Wynne Stadium, beating the Edmonton Eskimos in a 43-37 comeback. The lead changed six times during the game and the final outcome wasn't decided until cornerback Adrion Smith picked off Danny McManus' pass with 1:33 left on the clock and raced 49 yards to the end zone.

The Argos followed up a year later by giving the fans their first back-to-back Grey Cups since the 1946 and '47 seasons. With Flutie again leading the way, the Argos demolished the Saskatchewan Roughriders 47-23 in the final.

The Boatmen were undoubtedly the class of the CFL, but they still couldn't sell themselves beyond their loyal core of fans. Average attendance during the regular season was only slightly over 18,000 and it seemed impossible that the team would be able to retain Flutie, who was starting to receive overtures from NFL teams that had rejected him when he graduated from Boston College a decade earlier.

Sure enough, Flutie left for a long-awaited NFL opportunity with the Buffalo Bills and leaks began to appear once again in the Boatmen's hull. Matthews left after a mediocre 9-9 record in 1998 and, after a similar showing the next season with Jim Barker wearing the coach's whistle, TSN sold the club to New York businessman Sherwood Schwarz.

Right Doug Flutie (1996-97) readies to fire.

Out of the gloom there appeared a faint light of hope

The circus was about to return to town.

Schwarz would later confess that he was convinced to buy the team by his cousin J.I. Albrecht, who had been associated with a number of CFL teams, including a stint with the Argos in the early '70s as a scout. On Albrecht's advice, Schwarz hired John Huard, who had coached the Shreveport Pirates for a short spell during the U.S. expansion, and that turned out to be a disaster as most observers had predicted. By mid-season Huard resigned after a 51-4 drubbing by the B.C. Lions in front of a record-low 11,350.

Out of the gloom, however, there appeared a faint light of hope. Clemons, undoubtedly the most popular player to wear the Double Blue, was nearing the end of a brilliant 12-year career. In an attempt to salvage what was rapidly turning into a putrid mess, Clemons was asked to hang up his helmet and don the head coach's cap. He initially hesitated but then, in August 2000, agreed to accept the daunting task.

FAN MEMORY

BY ETHAN BARNES

As a fourth generation Argos fan, I've been going to team events as long as I can remember. (I'm 12.) A favourite moment took place three years ago during fan day.

After a thrilling practice with the players, I got to meet Coach Pinball. He asked me, along with another boy, Alex, what positions we played. I quickly answered wide receiver, while Alex said quarterback.

Incredibly, Pinball then called for a football and invited us to show him what we could do. We proceeded to run a couple of plays, after which he asked for *our* autographs, to post in his office. We proudly obliged.

He then announced to everyone gathered that we were now Argonauts' property; that this was one of the team's "secret recruitment techniques." Pinball told us to remember when we become draft eligible that we're already spoken for.

I'll remember, as from then I'll always be Double Blue!

Left Racing to make new Argo friends.

"To me, hiring him is the least risky of the alternatives," said Schwarz. "He's very, very smart and he has 12 years in the league."

It turned out to be one of several moves Schwarz would make. He fired Albrecht and hired outgoing CFL president Jeff Giles as team president and Paul Masotti, who had retired after the 1999 season, as general manager. Clemons stayed on as head coach in 2001 and also took on the title of vice president.

The shake-up, however, didn't do much for the team's fortunes on the field or at the turnstiles. Only 11,041 fans showed for the team's second home game of the season, a loss to the Winnipeg Blue Bombers. The Argos would go on to finish last in the East once again and Giles quit as president, paving the way for Clemons to take over that position and hand the whistle and clipboard to defensive coordinator Gary Etcheverry to start the 2002 season.

But by mid-term Clemons found himself once again exchanging his suit and tie for a coach's garb. Taking over a team that had managed just four wins in its first 12 games, Clemons rallied them to four victories in their final six matches and a second-place finish in the dismal East Division, where only the first-place Alouettes would have a winning record.

Mike Morreale, 1995-96, 2002-03.

The Argos beat cross-over Saskatchewan Roughriders in the semi-final to advance to the division final for the first time since 1997. And while they were beaten by Montreal, Clemons continued to show that he could be a winning coach. He followed up in 2003 with a 9-9 record and another victory in the semi-final, this time over B.C., before losing again to Montreal in the division final.

Before the season ended, the CFL assumed control of the club from Schwarz, paving the way for another ownership change. But this time the Argos fell into the hands of the capable stewardship of Howard Sokolowski and David Cynamon.

~ RICK MATSUMOTO

Images 1991-2003

Above Argos celebrate with fans after their 1991 Grey Cup win.

Left Bruce McNall and Wayne Gretzky on the sidelines.

Opposite Pinball Clemons on the move.

TRACY HAM ESCAPES THE POCKET

PAUL MASOTTI CELEBRATES

ROBERT CLARK BRINGS IT IN, 1993

KEN BENSON, 1992-93 & 1996-97

HARAROLD HALLMAN, 1988-93

Top Right Pinball Clemons, Robert Drummond and Mookie Mitchell, 1997.

Above Michael Fletcher, 2002-present.

Right Jock Climie, 1990 & 1995.

Left Demetrious Maxie, 1996-99 & 2002.

Below Kent Austin (1995) and daughter Kendall.

Bottom Ed Berry, 1988-92 & 1996.

CHAMPIONS

Left 1996 Grey Cup champions celebrate in the snow in Hamilton.

Top Doug Flutie and head coach Don Matthews in the 1997 Grey Cup Parade.

Above Mike Vanderjagt kicks as Flutie holds, 1997.

Left Kerwin Bell, 1998 & 2000-01.

Below Robert Drummond, 1996-97 & 2002.

Bottom Adrion "Pee Wee" Smith, 1996-2005.

Out of the gloom, however, there appeared a faint light of hope

Left Mike O'Shea, 1996-99 & 2001-present.

Top Right Michael Bishop, 2002-present.

Above Sandy Annunziata, 1999-2004.

Left The young faithful.

Below A Charlie Brown moment by Argos' mascot Scully.

Bottom Equipment maestros Danny Webb and Jason Colero.

Opposite page, top Bravely flying the colours at Ivor Wynne Stadium.

Opposite page, right Give us an "A

Opposite page, bottom Chris Schultz instructing his broadcast colleague James Duthie.

96
ARRRGOO
TICATS
SUCK

A

CHAMPIONS
66
LIGHT

Return to Glory

SECTION 7

7

2004–2006

CFL
ARGOS
Riddell

The Argos rejuvenation began in late 2003 with the introduction of David

Cynamon and Howard Sokolowski as the club's new owners. "The new owners are Torontonians actively engaged in their community and passionate about the Canadian game and their new team," said CFL Commissioner Tom Wright, the man instrumental in recruiting the two local businessmen.

The Argonauts organization gained instant credibility when they announced on the same day that Keith Pelley was leaving The Sports Network (TSN) to become the new President and CEO of the Toronto Argonauts.

The organization's rise back to respectability began early under Pelley's tenure. He sought to make the Argonauts Toronto's community team. Several programmes were launched and the innovative *See you on the Field* became more than a slogan as fans were allowed onto the turf at the end of home games to interact with the players.

The Argonauts made headlines early in the new regime signing free-agent star running back John Avery. Coming off a leg injury, Avery just missed rushing for 1,000 yards in his first season in Toronto.

The Argos made another splash in the free agency market in September in an attempt to beef up for the playoffs, winning a bidding war against several teams for the services of receiver Arland Bruce III. Bruce paid immediate dividends on both offence and special teams but it

Left New Argos president Keith Pelley (left) and owners David Cynamon and Howard Sokolowski are welcomed to the fold by then CFL Commissioner Tom Wright, 2003.

Previous page Jonathan Brown gives Jude St. John a champagne shower to celebrate the Argonauts' 15th Grey Cup title, 2004.

> Damon Allen, the game MVP, was brilliant

was in the playoffs where he truly shone. He scored two touchdowns in the East final, including one on a 97-yard kickoff return, leading the Argos back to the Grey Cup for the first time since 1997.

But the road to the 2004 Grey Cup had been anything but smooth. The Argonauts suffered a setback in August when starting quarterback Damon Allen was diagnosed with an undisplaced fracture of his left tibia as a result of a hit incurred in a game in Montreal. Michael Bishop emerged as Allen's replacement and guided the team to a winning record in Allen's absence.

The underdog Argos were a relaxed bunch leading up to the Grey Cup game against the B.C. Lions in Ottawa. The mood at kickoff was electric. Under coach Michael Clemons, the Argos had proven all season to be a resilient bunch. B.C. scored on their opening drive but Toronto came to life and led 17-10 at the half.

Damon Allen, the game MVP, was brilliant. He sealed the Lions' fate early in the third quarter when he marched the Argos downfield for another touchdown and a 24-10 lead. A Lions' comeback fell short and the Argos won 27-19.

How unexpected was this Grey Cup victory? Most of the Argos staff was in its first year with the club. Following the parade and rally at City Hall, the Grey Cup was returned to the Argos' team offices at SkyDome in the backseat of a crammed car. Inside, a group of staff members debated what to do with the trophy.

As one employee recalled, "What do we do with it now? I guess we should lock it up."

In preparing for the final, there had been a game plan, a travel plan, and a parade plan. But no Grey Cup plan. In the end, the trophy spent the night locked inside the Argonauts' executive offices.

The 2004 season was truly magical. More than 26,000 fans filled the SkyDome for the opening game of the new regime and more than 37,000 people, the largest crowd since 1992, packed the Dome to watch the Argos and Tiger-Cats in the East semi-final. The Argonauts had returned to the mainstream of the Toronto sports scene.

Heading into the 2005 season, with all 24 starters from 2004 under

Top John Feugill and Damon Allen, selected the game's MVP, salute the fans following their 2004 Grey Cup win.

Above Allen (left) with brothers Harold and Pro Football Hall of Famer Marcus.

Left Mike O'Shea (1996-99 & 2001-present), Chad Folk (1997-present) and Jude St. John (1998-present) savour victory.

ARGO MEMORY

MICHAEL CLEMONS

My most memorable experience as an Argonaut was winning the 2004 Grey Cup.

As a player I had won it three times, but as coach I felt I won it 40 times—once for every player on the team.

That feeling came over me as I watched the players receiving the Grey Cup from Commissioner Tom Wright after we defeated the B.C. Lions at Frank Clair Stadium in Ottawa.

I was standing at the bottom of the stairs to the stage where the trophy presentation was to take place. I was doing an interview with a reporter, who said to me "You'd better hurry (onto the stage) because they're about to present the Cup." But I had already told Beth Waldman (Argos' media relations director) that the captains would receive it. So I told the reporter, "You can keep asking me questions because the Grey Cup is not about me, it's not about the coaches, it's about the players."

It was a beautiful, crisp fall night and when the glitter (large pieces of confetti) went up and you saw all the guys with the Grey Cup. It was like a movie. It was like watching something outside of yourself.

I could see the sense of pride and accomplishment in their faces and it made me feel so great to be a part of what they had achieved.

The Grey Cup is not about me, it's not about the coaches, it's about the players

contract, expectations for a Grey Cup repeat were high. The year began with an historic pre-season game played on the campus of Saint Mary's University in Halifax in front of a sold-out crowd. This was the first time that a CFL game was held in Halifax and the Argonauts and Hamilton Tiger-Cats played to a 16-16 draw.

The Argos went 11-7 and won the East Division for the first time since 1997. The biggest story, though, was the play of Allen. Despite turning 41 midway through the season, Allen had his most productive year as a professional, surpassing the 5,000-yard passing plateau for the first time in his storied career. He was named the CFL's all-star quarterback and was overwhelmingly voted as the CFL's Most Outstanding Player.

But the Argonauts regular season success didn't carry into the playoffs. The visiting Montreal Alouettes enacted some revenge from the previous season with a 33-17 upset victory. The season was deemed to have ended prematurely for the Boatmen who were favoured to return to the Grey Cup on the strength of their defence and Allen's rejuvenated form.

Off the field, the Argonauts continued to make inroads in the

FAN MEMORY
BY PETER VASOFF

After the 2004 Grey Cup game in Ottawa, I found out where the Argos were staying and went there to congratulate the players after their victory over B.C. I never expected to get past the lobby but the fans were invited to the Argos party room, with the stipulation that seats at tables were reserved for the team and their families.

We were also invited to help ourselves at the buffet bar. I mingled with the players and Mike O'Shea autographed my No. 50 jersey. Later, I was able to hold the Grey Cup (good thing Mario Vespa was not there) and got a picture.

Since then the Argos have led me across this great country of ours. From Halifax to Vancouver with stops in Edmonton, Calgary, Regina, Winnipeg, Hamilton, Ottawa, Montreal, and last but not least, Toronto.

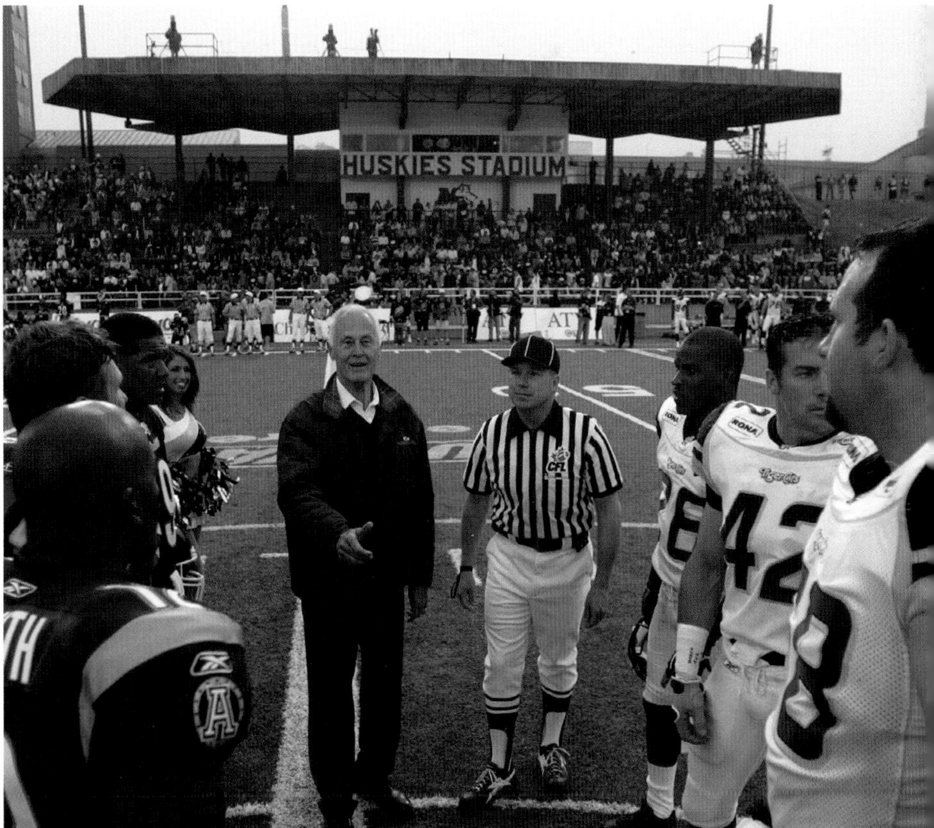

Right Pre-season game at Huskies Stadium in Halifax, 2005.

community, launching the Argos Foundation – Stop the Violence campaign in August to help combat a rise in violent crime.

Amidst considerable fanfare, Ricky Williams was introduced

The Argonauts averaged more than 30,000 fans for the first time since 1992. Given the success of the football club, Sports Media Canada named co-owners Howard Sokolowski and David Cynamon the Magna International's Sports Executives of the Year. On November 16th, the CFL announced that the 95th Grey Cup would be played at the Rogers Centre (formerly SkyDome). This marked a return to the original city of the Grey Cup and the first time Canada's premier sporting event would be played in Toronto since 1992.

The 95th Grey Cup is billed as a Celebration of Football involving high school and university football championships, and marking the first time that both the Grey Cup and the Vanier Cup were scheduled in the same city on the same weekend.

The Argonauts stayed in the headlines during the early months of 2006. In mid-February, the team inked former Heisman Trophy winner Eric Crouch. Two months later, suspended Miami Dolphins running back Ricky Williams was added to the club's negotiation list and rumours began to swirl of another Heisman Trophy winner joining the Double Blue.

FAN MEMORY

BY JOHN ROBINSON

I have many memories of times spent with the Argos but the one that meant the most to me involved my son. Lucas, 12, lives with his mom in Newfoundland and comes to visit each summer. His favourite time here is when we go the Argos game, where we are season ticket holders.

After the game on July 8th, Lucas and I went down on the field to see one of his favourite players, Clifford Ivory. I caught Clifford's eye and he brought us into the family section, which made Lucas feel like a VIP. When Lucas asked if there were other players he could approach for autographs, Clifford suggested we attend a practice where it would be less busy.

We attended a practice a couple of weeks later. Lucas was trying to catch Clifford's eye when Clifford saw him and called out, "Hey, Lucas." For Lucas, that was a very special moment. Excited, he said, "Dad, Cliff knows my name!" This may seem like a small thing to some but to Lucas it meant the world.

Right Clifford Ivory (2002-06).

Early on the morning of Sunday, May 28th, the Argonauts called a press conference. Amidst considerable fanfare, Ricky Williams was introduced to the media in a jam-packed conference room at the Rogers Centre. The interest in Williams by fans and media followed him wherever he went. But Williams had trouble adjusting to the Canadian game and suffered a broken arm during a July road game in Regina. He returned to the lineup late in the season and found some success lining up as a fullback in front of John Avery.

The month of May saw the end of one of the most prolific careers in Argonauts' history when the longest serving member of the team and three-time Grey Cup champion Adrion Smith announced his retirement.

On the field, the 2006 season proved to be one of milestones. Long-time Argo Mike O'Shea recorded his 1,000th career tackle becoming the first Canadian to reach that mark and only the third player to do so in CFL history. Byron Parker emerged with a record-setting performance for the most interception return yards in a season.

But the biggest milestone was reached by Allen. He missed four games after injuring a finger in the season opener, but quickly regained his 2005 form and his assault on professional football's all-time passing list. On September 5th in Hamilton, Allen completed a 29-yard shovel pass to Arland Bruce III. Bruce scored on the play and Allen surpassed Warren Moon's record of 70,553 career

FAN MEMORY

BY KEVIN GILLEN

Having spent all of my 46 years living in and around Toronto, and being a huge football fan, I have spent many exciting afternoons cheering on the Argos. But the one day that will forever stick out was May 6, 2006.

That was the day that my eldest son, Connor, 11 at the time, attended an Argos Youth Camp. The camp was everything we expected and so much more. Upwards of 60 boys aged 12 to 16 participated in clinics enthusiastically run by many of the 2006 Toronto Argonauts.

My son's clinics were run by No. 97 Jonathan Brown. The following week, Connor changed his position to defensive end. He went on to win numerous awards on his atom football team and now proudly wears his No. 97 Argos jersey wherever and whenever he can.

Right Connor and Jonathan Brown (2004-06).

Top Arland Bruce III pulls one down against the Alouettes, 2006.

Right Celebrating Damon Allen's ascension as the pro game's all-time leading passer.

Far right Howard Sokolowski, Ricky Williams and David Cynamon, 2006.

Below Michael Bishop bulls for a first down, 2006.

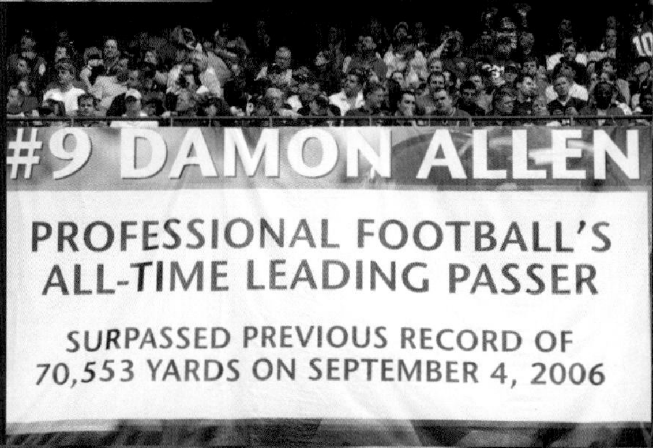

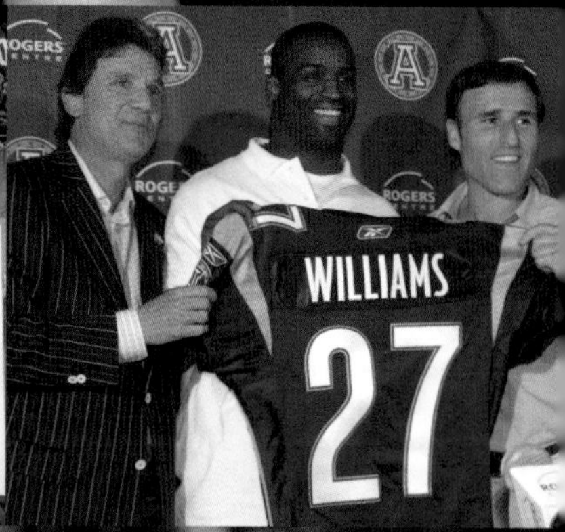

passing yards.

It was an up-and-down year for the Boatmen. They started the season 2-5 before winning five straight and eight of nine contests to grab first place in the East Division, and then losing first place following back-to-back home losses to close out the season.

Toronto hosted the upstart Winnipeg Blue Bombers in the East semi-final. Trailing 27-17 late in the fourth quarter, back-up quarterback Michael Bishop tossed a pair of fourth-quarter touchdown passes to lead the Argonauts to victory. However, the Boatmen fell 33-24 to the Montreal Alouettes the following week in the East championship.

Following the season, Keith Pelley was named #16 on the *Globe and Mail*'s list of the Top 25 most influential people in Canadian sport. Under his leadership and the commitment of a pair of local owners the future remains bright for the Argonauts heading into the 2007 season as the Grey Cup game makes a triumphant return to the City of Toronto.

~ JAIME STEIN

FAN MEMORY

BY JAKE RANOT

I was almost eight years old. My dad took me and my friend, David, to the Argos open practice on Fan Day.

David and I were watching Damon Allen and the back-up quarterback throw passes. The back-up quarterback saw me and David and told us to get in line behind the receivers. We stood behind Robert Baker.

When it was our turn, the quarterback threw passes to us and we each caught it! I know he threw it softly but it was a great feeling to catch a ball thrown by a CFL quarterback on the big field with the yard line markers on it.

The quarterback was Marcus Brady and I was sad when he got traded to Hamilton next season.

My dad and I went to Ottawa to see the Argos beat B.C. in the 2004 Grey Cup. I guess that should be my greatest memory as an Argo fan but David and I still talk about how cool it was to catch those passes.

Right Marcus Brady (2002-03)

Right Antonious Bonner hauls down the Als' Anthony Cavillo, 2006.

Below Kevin Eiben guns for the Stamps' Henry Burris, 2006.

FAN MEMORY

BY DALE GERMAIN

My favourite Argo memory goes back only a couple of years.

We were in Ottawa for the Grey Cup in 2004 and had seats in the end zone on the Texas Lone Star Grill Deck. We sat right in the middle and could almost touch the field from where we were.

After we won the game, Tony Miles came by our seats and slapped hands with us in celebration.

What a moment! To see my Argos win the Grey Cup and share a moment with one of our great receivers, it was the highlight of my football life.

Right Tony Miles, 2003-present.

TORONTO ARGONAUTS SONG

Go Toronto Argos go go go
Pull together fight the foe foe foe
Scoring touchdowns for the blue on blue
The Argos will win for you

Full of fight and courage you can't stop
They pile up the points until they reach
the top
Pull together till the Grey Cup's won
Go Argos go go go

INSTRUMENTAL BREAK

Go Toronto Argos go go go
Pull together fight the foe foe foe
Scoring touchdowns for the blue on blue
The Argos will win for you

Full of fight and courage you can't stop
They pile up the points until they reach
the top
Pull together till the Grey Cup's won
Go Argos go Toronto go
Go Argos go go go

FAN MEMORY

BY MALCOLM WILHELM

I may be young but I am and will always be an Argos fan. My Argos memory isn't a Grey Cup victory or a big play, it was just good old football.

I went to see the September 30, 2006 game against Calgary. I had to go alone. I would have liked to go with a friend but I couldn't. I had won the pair of tickets in a contest. They were fairly good seats, but since it was just me, I traded them for one ticket on the 50-yard line. Best experience of my life.

I thought the Argos could win even though we lost to Calgary the week before. Well, even though I was alone I made an unusual friend, another young Argos fan, and after the Argos got their first touchdown we just connected. I offered to buy him a drink and he bought me some popcorn. We just clicked; maybe it was just the emotion of the game, but it was great. Two touchdowns, it was an exciting game, we won the game and emotion was in the air.

Well, that would have to be my fondest memory with the Argos. I went to see a game and I made a good friend who to this day I still talk to.

FAN MEMORY

BY MIKE BLUMBERG

Being a huge Argos fan my entire (and short) 24 years, thanks to my dad, I had to get my girlfriend Alyssa involved with the excitement.

We started by watching a few games on the TV together Friday and Saturday nights, which shortly turned to her watching *all* the televised games with me (even if we were out). Alyssa started getting more and more involved with the game, wanting to learn more and more of what's happening on the field.

I took her to her first Argos home game and she just *loved* it. She had a blast. Since then we have been to countless home games together and *always* have a great time. So when the day came to ask her to marry me, I could only think of one way to make it special, different and *ours*—AT THE ARGOS GAME!

On Saturday, September 9, 2006, nine minutes into the first quarter, I got down on my knee and popped the question. After the shock and happiness settled, Alyssa said yes (thank God) in front of 32,000 screaming Argos fans. For the rest of the day everyone knew who we were, it was our 15 minutes of fame. It was the *best* game we have ever attended, and will be the most special day for us for the rest of our lives.

Thank you Toronto Argonauts!

Left Noel Prefontaine, 1998-present.

FAN MEMORY

BY CHRISTINE BOOMHOUR

My favourite memory had to do with my dad. He passed away September 15, 2006 and was a die-hard Argos fan. He was the one that got me into football and loving the Argos as much as I do.

He took me to my first Argos game and tried so hard to get me to understand the game. But try as he might, I never did get it—but now I do!

The look on his face when the Argos won a Grey Cup, or just a game, will always stay with me. My sister and I had bought an Argos jacket for dad for his 75th birthday and he never took it off. Now I am the proud owner of that jacket and never take it off!

Just sharing the stories about the past played game with dad will always stick in my head. The way how he would have done it if he were coach always made me laugh. But he loved his team through thick or thin.

Above John Avery reverses field against the Renegades, 2005.

Left Bashir Levingston on the move against the Ticats, 2006.

Right Michael Fletcher, 2002-present.

Far right Kenny Wheaton (2003-present) en route to his record 116-yard interception return in the East semi-final, 2004.

Below Eric England, 2003-06.

Below right Andre Talbot, 2001-present.

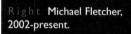

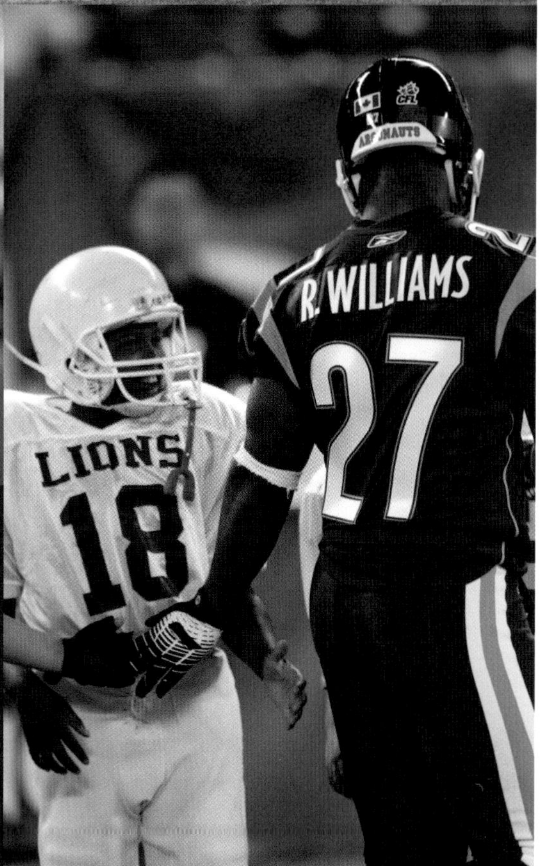

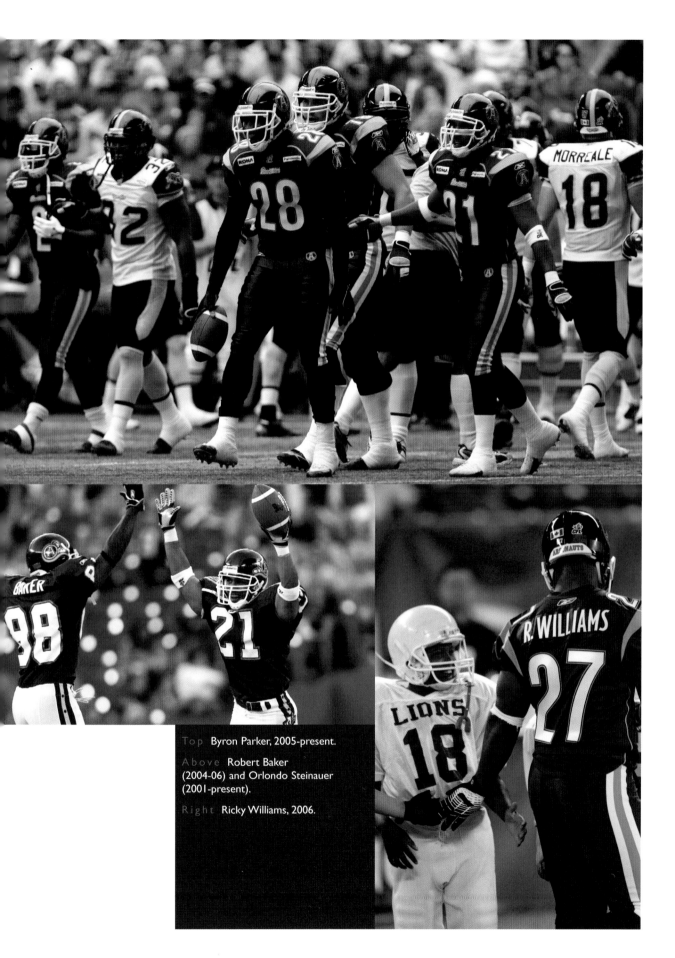

Top Byron Parker, 2005-present.

Above Robert Baker (2004-06) and Orlondo Steinauer (2001-present).

Right Ricky Williams, 2006.

PRESENTED
AMATEUR RUGBY

SECTION 8

Appendix 8

ALL-TIME ARGONAUTS

The Banner hanging from the rafters of the Rogers Centre symbolizes the 19 All-Time Argonauts.

#	Name	Year
55	Joe Krol	1996
22	Dick Shatto	1996
60	Danny Nykoluk	1996
33	Bill Symons	1996
10	Terry Greer	1996
77	Royal Copeland	1997
79	Jim Corrigall	1997
67	Teddy Morris	1988
27	Marv Luster	1998
7	Condredge Holloway	1998
36	Don Moen	1999
66	Bill Zock	1999
88	Paul Masotti	2000
31	Michael Clemons	2000
52	Les Ascott	2004
20	Jim Rountree	2004
16	Dave Mann	2005
81	Ulysses Curtis	2005
69	Dan Ferrone	2006

RETIRED JERSEYS

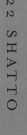

22 SHATTO

31 CLEMONS

55 KROL

60 NYKOLUK

All-Time Argonauts Grey Cup Rosters

1911

University of Toronto 14 : Argonauts 7 Coach : Billy Foulds

PLAYER	POSITION	PLAYER	POSITION	PLAYER	POSITION	PLAYER	POSITION
Smith, Everett	FB	Russell, Fred	OL	Moore, Bert	Wing	Lockhart, Eugene	Sub
Binkley, Ross	HB	Kent, Mert	OL	Murray, Mac	Wing	Parks, John	Sub
Mallett, Billy	HB	Murphy, Glad	Wing	Addison, Gander	Sub	Wright, George	Sub
Lawson, Smirle	HB	Gale, Beecher	Wing	Bancroft, A.	Sub		
O'Connor, Jack	QB	Arnoldt, Franquir	Wing	Brown, William	Sub		
Sinclair, Aleck	OL	Wigle, Rajah	Wing	Jarvis, William	Sub		

1912

Hamilton Alerts 11 : Argonauts 4 Coach : Jack Newton

PLAYER	POSITION	PLAYER	POSITION	PLAYER	POSITION	PLAYER	POSITION
Meigham, Tom	Wing	Grey, Paul	OL	Sinclair, Aleck	Wing	Clarke, Crossen	Sub
Lawson, Smirle	HB	Mulligan, Murray	OL	Heuther, Dutch	Wing	Murphy, Jimmy	Sub
Binkley, Ross	HB	Murphy, Glad	OL	Murray, Mac	Wing	Patterson, Pat	Sub
O'Connor, Jack	HB	Galt	Wing	Reaume, Stanley	Wing	Price, Cecil	Sub
Dissette, Jimmy	QB	Foster, Frank	Wing	Addison, Gander	Sub		

1914

Argonauts 14 : University of Toronto 2 Coach : Billy Foulds

PLAYER	POSITION	PLAYER	POSITION	PLAYER	POSITION	PLAYER	POSITION
Murphy, Glad	Wing	Patterson, Pat	OL	Burkart, Babe	Wing	Heuther, Dutch	Sub
Lawson, Smirle	HB	Davison, Bobby	OL	Murray, Gordon	Wing	Lepper, B.	Sub
Smith, Everett	HB	Simpson, Collin	OL	Knight, Frank	Wing	Lobraico, J.	Sub
O'Connor, Jack	HB	McFarlane, Alex	Wing	Dibble, Bob	Sub	McDonald, M.P.	Sub
Holmes, Wendell	HB	Foster, Frank	Wing	Duke, Hermis	Sub	Simpson, Ben	Sub
Mills, Freddie	QB	Motley, Arthur	Wing	Gonter, Matt	Sub	Smith, George "Kid"	Sub

1920

University of Toronto 16 : Argonauts 3 Coach : Mike Rodden

PLAYER	POSITION	PLAYER	POSITION	PLAYER	POSITION	PLAYER	POSITION
Gilhooley, Walter	Wing	Shoebottom, Lionel	OL	Grey, Paul	Wing	Murphy, Jimmy	Sub
Munro, Dunc	HB	Sinclair, Aleck	OL	Britnell, Gordon	Wing	Park, Alex	Sub
O'Connor, Jack	HB	Sullivan, Frank	Wing	Fear, Cap	Sub	Pugh, Harold	Sub
Batstone, Harry	HB	Hay, J.S.	Wing	Garrett, Doug	Sub	Young, Bunny	Sub
Cochrane, Shrimp	QB	Heustis, Doug	Wing	Henderson	Sub		
Polson, Bobby	OL	Romeril, Alex	Wing	Laurie, Doug	Sub		

1921

Argonauts 23 : Edmonton Eskimos 0 Coach : Sinc McEvenue

PLAYER	POSITION	PLAYER	POSITION	PLAYER	POSITION	PLAYER	POSITION
Stirrett, Jo Jo	Wing	Hay, J.S.	Wing	Burkart, Babe	Sub	Sinclair, Aleck	Sub
Batstone, Harry	HB	Romeril, Alex	Wing	Burt, Milt	Sub	Sullivan, Frank	Sub
Conacher, Lionel	HB	Earle, Hap	Wing	Clarke, Tommy	Sub	Thom, Gord	Sub
McCormack, Moss	HB	Fear, Cap	Wing	Heustis, Doug	Sub	Wallace, Laurie	Sub
Cochrane, Shrimp	QB	Britnell, Gordon	Wing	MacKenzie, Red	Sub	Young, Bunny	Sub
Douglas, Jimmy	Snap	Abbott, Don	Sub	Polson, Bobby	Sub		
Sullivan, Glenn	Wing	Bradfield, Babe	Sub	Pugh, Harold	Sub		

1933

Argonauts 4 : Sarnia Imperials 3 Coach : Lew Hayman

PLAYER	POSITION	PLAYER	POSITION	PLAYER	POSITION	PLAYER	POSITION
Smith, Jack	Wing	Wright, Joe	Snap	Cutler, Wes	Wing	Staughton, Len	Sub
Box, Ab	HB	Palmer, Jim	Wing	Moore, Whitney	Wing	Stevenson, Frank	Sub
Taylor, Jack	HB	McNichol, Baz	Wing	Griffiths, Tuffy	Sub	Upper, Art	Sub
Morris, Teddy	HB	Burns, Tommy	Wing	Miller, Whitey	Sub	Vail, Red	Sub
Mullan, Andy	QB	Tindall, Frank	Wing	Munro, Armour	Sub	Wilson, W.F.	Sub

1937

Argonauts 4 : Winnipeg Blue Bombers 3 Coach : Lew Hayman

PLAYER	POSITION	PLAYER	POSITION	PLAYER	POSITION	PLAYER	POSITION
Morris, Teddy	Wing	Barker, Reg	Snap	Cutler, Wes	Wing	Miller, Joe	Sub
West, Art	HB	Palmer, Jim	Wing	Bryers, Bill	Wing	Selkirk, Earl	Sub
Isbister, Bob	HB	Staughton, Len	Wing	Deadey, Leo	Sub	Storey, Red	Sub
MacPherson, Doug	HB	Burt, Clary	Wing	Edwards, Jake	Sub	Vail, Red	Sub
Stukus, Bill	QB	Evans, Art	Wing	Ferris, Dave	Sub	Young, Jack	Sub

1938

Argonauts 30 : Winnipeg Blue Bombers 7 Coach : Lew Hayman

PLAYER	POSITION	PLAYER	POSITION	PLAYER	POSITION	PLAYER	POSITION
Morris, Teddy	Wing	Hees, George	Snap	Cutler, Wes	Wing	Reid, Pat	Sub
Wes, Art	HB	Palmer, Jim	Wing	Thornton, Bernie	Wing	Selkirk, Earl	Sub
Isbister, Bob	HB	Staughton, Len	Wing	Levantis, Steve	Sub	Storey, Red	Sub
MacPherson, Doug	HB	Burt, Clary	Wing	McLean, Chuck	Sub	Stukus, Annis	Sub
Stukus, Bill	QB	Evans, Art	Wing	Miller, Joe	Sub	Wedley, Jack	Sub

1945

Argonauts 35 : Winnipeg Blue Bombers 0 Coach : Ted Morris

PLAYER	POSITION	PLAYER	POSITION	PLAYER	POSITION	PLAYER	POSITION
Skidmore, Art	Wing	Zock, Bill	Wing	Curtin, Bob	Sub	Pruski, Steve	Sub
Smylie, Doug	HB	Ascott, Les	Wing	Goyer, Vern	Sub	Richardson, Bruce	Sub
Copeland, Royal	HB	Levantis, Steve	Wing	Hickey, Red	Sub	Waldon, Tom	Sub
Karrys, Byron	HB	Cassidy, Leonard	Wing	Karrys, Steve	Sub	Tommy, Andy	Sub
Doty, Fred	QB	Wedley, Jack	Wing	Krol, Joe	Sub		
Glenn, Tom	Snap	Bell, Billy	Sub	Leeming, Jack	Sub		
Morris, Frank	Wing	Carr-Harris, Phil	Sub	Myers, Billy	Sub		

1946

Argonauts 28 : Winnipeg Blue Bombers 6 Coach : Ted Morris

PLAYER	POSITION	PLAYER	POSITION	PLAYER	POSITION	PLAYER	POSITION
Karrys, Steve	Wing	Morris, Frank	Wing	Camilleri, Chuck	Sub	Robinson, Don	Sub
Karrys, Byron	HB	Zock, Bill	Wing	Courtney, Ted	Sub	Santucci, Pat	Sub
Krol, Joe	HB	Ascott, Les	Wing	Deadey, Leo	Sub	Smylie, Rod	Sub
Copeland, Royal	HB	Levantis, Steve	Wing	Glenn, Tom	Sub	Tipoff, Boris	Sub
Bell, Billy	QB	Reid, Pat	Wing	Grice, Hal	Sub	Titanic, Pete	Sub
Loney, Don	Snap	Wedley, Jack	Wing	Levantis, John	Sub	West, Art	Sub

1947

Argonauts 10 : Winnipeg Blue Bombers 9 Coach : Ted Morris

PLAYER	POSITION	PLAYER	POSITION	PLAYER	POSITION	PLAYER	POSITION
McKay, Bob	Wing	Morris, Frank	Wing	Briggs, Bill	Sub	Meen, George	Sub
Copeland, Royal	HB	Zock, Bill	Wing	Brown, Doug	Sub	Pyzer, Doug	Sub
Krol, Joe	HB	Ascott, Les	Wing	Cassidy, Leonard	Sub	Reid, Pat	Sub
Karrys, Byron	HB	Levantis, Steve	Wing	Fleet, Eric	Sub	Robinson, Don	Sub
Doty, Fred	QB	Titanic, Pete	Wing	Grass, Rudy	Sub	Stukus, Bill	Sub
Turner, Doug	Snap	Wedley, Jack	Wing	Hazel, Bob	Sub	Turnbull, Ken	Sub

1950

Argonauts 13 : Winnipeg Blue Bombers 0 Coach : Frank Clair

PLAYER	POSITION	PLAYER	POSITION	PLAYER	POSITION	PLAYER	POSITION
Smylie, Rod	Wing	McCormick, Bill	G	Dunlap, Jake	Sub	Titanic, Pete	Sub
Curtis, Ulysses	HB	Kerns, John	T	Fowler, Bud	Sub	Volpe, Nick	Sub
Bass, Billy	HB	Parkin, Lorne	T	Karrys, Byron	Sub	Wedley, Jack	Sub
Toogood, Ted	HB	Scott, Don	E	Krol, Joe	Sub	Westlake, Bob	Sub
Dekdebrun, Al	QB	Whaley, Marv	E	McKenzie, Shanty	Sub		
Hirsch, Ed	C	Ascott, Les	Sub	Shore, Johnny	Sub		
Black, Fred	G	Bennett, Pete	Sub	Stocks, Arnie	Sub		

1952

Argonauts 21 : Edmonton Eskimos 11 Coach : Frank Clair

PLAYER	POSITION	PLAYER	POSITION	PLAYER	POSITION	PLAYER	POSITION
Smylie, Rod	Wing	McKenzie, Shanty	G	Copeland, Royal	Sub	Scullion, Art	Sub
Bass, Billy	HB	Carpenter, Jack	T	Gray, Jack	Sub	Shore, Johnny	Sub
Pyzer, Doug	HB	Parkin, Lorne	T	Harpley, Tom	Sub	Smylie, Doug	Sub
Curtis, Ulysses	HB	Bruno, Al	E	Karrys, Steve	Sub	Soergel, Ed	Sub
Wirkowski, Nobby	QB	O'Connor, Zeke	E	Krol, Joe	Sub	Toogood, Ted	Sub
Ettinger, Red	C	Ascott, Les	Sub	Marshall, Bob	Sub		
Black, Fred	G	Bennett, Pete	Sub	Roberts, Jack	Sub		

1971

Calgary Stampeders 14 : Argonauts 11 Coach : Leo Cahill

PLAYER	POSITION	PLAYER	POSITION	PLAYER	POSITION	PLAYER	POSITION
Henderson, Jim	E	Theismann, Joe	QB	Wells, George	DL	Luster, Marv	DB
Profit, Mel	E	Barton, Greg	QB	Corrigall, Jim	DL	Barrett, Larry	DB
Moro, Tony	E	Desjardins, Paul	OL	Knechtel, Dave	DL	Anderson, Tim	DB
Eben, Mike	FL	Bray, Charles	OL	Vijuk, Joe	DL	Raimey, Dave	DB
McQuay, Leon	B	Scales, Roger	OL	Brame, Larry	LB	Thorton, Dick	DB
Symons, Bill	B	Nykoluk, Danny	OL	Mack, Gene	LB	Paquette, Peter	DB
Cranmer, Dave	B	Kelly, Ellison	OL	Aldridge, Dick	LB	Andrusyshyn, Zenon	P
Abofs, Harry	B	Stillwagon, Jim	DL	Martin, Peter	LB	MacMillan, Ivan	K

1982

Edmonton Eskimos 32 : Argonauts 16 Coach : Bob O'Billovich

PLAYER	POSITION	PLAYER	POSITION	PLAYER	POSITION	PLAYER	POSITION
Greer, Terry	WR	Barnes, Joe	QB	Lyszkiewicz, Leon	DL	Woods, Harold	DB
Tolbert, Emanuel	WR	Holloway, Condredge	QB	Mohr, Rick	DL	Wilson, Darrell	DB
Pearson, Paul	WR	Trifaux, Tom	OL	Olsen, Richard	DL	Heath, Jo Jo	DB
Newman, David	WR	Smith, Doug	OL	Del Col, Stephen	DL	Ackroyd, Steve	DB
Holmes, Greg	WR	Mangold, Roland	OL	Elser, Gordon	LB	Gray, Leo	DB
Minter, Cedric	RB	Malinosky, John	OL	Moen, Don	LB	Walker, Mervin	DB
Townsend, Geoff	RB	Ferrone, Dan	OL	Pointer, John	LB	Dorsey, Dean	P/K
Carinci, Jan	RB	Hameluck, Mike	OL	Berryman, Tim	LB		
Bronk, Bob	RB	Wilson, Earl	DL	Jackson, Ed	LB		

1983

Argonauts 18 : B.C. Lions 17 Coach : Bob O'Billovich

PLAYER	POSITION	PLAYER	POSITION	PLAYER	POSITION	PLAYER	POSITION
Greer, Terry	WR	Holloway, Condredge	QB	Del Col, Stephen	DL	Nicholson, Darrell	DB
Tolbert, Emanuel	WR	Trifaux, Tom	OL	King, Franklin	DL	Wilson, Darrell	DB
Pearson, Paul	WR	Ferrone, Dan	OL	Mohr, Rick	DL	Ackroyd, Steve	DB
Townsend, Geoff	WR	Antunovic, Tony	OL	Curry, James	LB	Brazley, Carl	DB
Holmes, Greg	WR	Hameluck, Mike	OL	Lawson, Tony	LB	Greene, Marcellus	DB
Minter, Cedric	RB	Malinosky, John	OL	Moen, Don	LB	Paul, Leroy	DB
Carinci, Jan	RB	Norton, Bill	OL	Elser, Gordon	LB	Ilesic, Hank	P/K
Palazeti, John	RB	Pruenster, Kelvin	DL	Mitchell, William	LB		
Barnes, Joe	QB	Wilson, Earl	DL	McEachern, Ken	DB		

1987

Edmonton Eskimos 38 : Argonauts 36 Coach : Bob O'Billovich

PLAYER	POSITION	PLAYER	POSITION	PLAYER	POSITION	PLAYER	POSITION
Smith, Darrell K.	WR	Renfroe, Gilbert	QB	Baylis, Jearld	DL	Daniels, David	DB
Thomas, Gene	WR	Schultz, Chris	OL	Harding, Rodney	DL	Vaughan, Jake	DB
Pearson, Paul	WR	Ferrone, Dan	OL	Kulka, Glen	DL	Drain, Selwyn	DB
Edwards, Dwight	WR	Beckstead, Ian	OL	Schmidt, Blaine	DL	Clash, Darnell	DB
Smith, Jeffrey	WR	Ambrosie, Randy	OL	Moen, Don	LB	Ryan, Rick	DB
Fenerty, Gil	RB	Pruenster, Kelvin	OL	Landry, Doug	LB	Ilesic, Hank	P
Johns, Tony	RB	Kardash, Jim	OL	Pless, Willie	LB	Chomyc, Lance	K
Hudson, Warren	RB	Skemp, Bob	OL	Elliott, Bruce	LB		
Barrett, Danny	QB	Sellers, Dan	DL	Pleasant, Reggie	DB		

1991

Argonauts 36 : Calgary Stampeders 21 Coach : Adam Rita

PLAYER	POSITION	PLAYER	POSITION	PLAYER	POSITION	PLAYER	POSITION
Williams, David	WR	Foggie, Rickey	QB	Harding, Rodney	DL	Bovell, Dave	DB
Ismail, Raghib	WR	Gillus, Willie	QB	Hallman, Harold	DL	Wilson, Don	DB
Masotti, Paul	WR	Schultz, Chris	OL	Warren, Brian	DL	Berry, Ed	DB
Smith, Darrell K.	WR	Ferrone, Dan	OL	Elliott, Bruce	DL	Rockford, James	DB
Murray, Andrew	WR	Beckstead, Ian	OL	Moen, Don	LB	VanBelleghem, Dave	DB
Izquierdo, J.P	WR	Skemp, Bob	OL	Gaines, Chris	LB	Ilesic, Hank	P
Clemons, Michael	RB	Pruenster, Kelvin	OL	Ford, Darryl	LB	Chomyc, Lance	K
Smellie, Kevin	RB	Kardash, Jim	OL	Castello, Keith	LB		
Nastasiuk, Paul	RB	Schimdt, Blaine	OL	Pleasant, Reggie	DB		
Dunigan, Matt	QB	Campbell, Mike	DL	Brazley, Carl	DB		

1996

Argonauts 43 : Edmonton Eskimos 37 Coach : Don Matthews

PLAYER	POSITION	PLAYER	POSITION	PLAYER	POSITION	PLAYER	POSITION
Masotti, Paul	WR	Flutie, Doug	QB	Cantor, Noah	DL	O'Shea, Mike	LB
Cunningham, James	WR	Fleetwood, Marquel	QB	Raposo, John	DL	Berry, Ed	DB
Williams, Tyrone	WR	Payne, Dan	OL	Stewart, Andrew	DL	Harris, Johnnie	DB
Dmytryshyn, Duane	WR	Gioskis, Chris	OL	Maxie, Demetrious	DL	Simmons, Marcello	DB
Morreale, Mike	WR	Vercheval, Pierre	OL	Waldrop, Rob	DL	Smith, Adrion	DB
Casola, Norm	WR	Perez, Chris	OL	Giles, Oscar	DL	Smith, Donald	DB
Drummond, Robert	RB	Kiselak, Mike	OL	Wilson, Don	LB	Nimako, George	DB
Clemons, Michael	RB	Stevenson, Vic	OL	Benson, Ken	LB	Smith, Lester	DB
Izquierdo, J.P.	RB	Givens, Reggie	DL	Harris, Cooper	LB	Vanderjagt, Mike	P/K

1997

Argonauts 47 : Saskatchewan Roughriders 23 Coach : Don Matthews

PLAYER	POSITION	PLAYER	POSITION	PLAYER	POSITION	PLAYER	POSITION
Masotti, Paul	WR	Ware, Andre	QB	Cantor, Noah	DL	O'Shea, Mike	LB
Mitchell, Derrell	WR	Payne, Dan	OL	Raposo, John	DL	Harris, Johnnie	DB
Dmytryshyn, Duane	WR	Gioskis, Chris	OL	Stewart, Andrew	DL	Simmons, Marcello	DB
Kirwan, Andre	WR	Vercheval, Pierre	OL	Maxie, Demetrious	DL	Bonner, Antonious	DB
Casola, Norm	WR	Kiselak, Mike	OL	Waldrop, Rob	DL	Smith, Adrion	DB
Montana, Denis	WR	Folk, Chad	OL	Wiltshire, Kelly	LB	Smith, Donald	DB
Drummond, Robert	RB	O'Day, Jeremy	OL	Johnson, Eric	LB	Nimako, George	DB
Clemons, Michael	RB	Williams, Willie	OL	Rogers, Brendan	LB	Smith, Lester	DB
Flutie, Doug	QB	Givens, Reggie	DL	Benson, Ken	LB	Vanderjagt, Mike	P/K

2004

Argonauts 27 : B.C. Lions 19 Coach : Michael Clemons

PLAYER	POSITION	PLAYER	POSITION	PLAYER	POSITION	PLAYER	POSITION
Bruce III, Arland	WR	Bishop, Michael	QB	Walsh, Chuck	DL	Srochenski, Randy	LB
Talbot, Andre	WR	Miller, Romaro	QB	Robinson, Gabe	DL	Steinauer, Orlondo	DB
Soward, R. Jay	WR	Folk, Chad	OL	England, Eric	DL	Hardy, Chris	DB
Miles, Tony	WR	Mihelic, Mike	OL	Brown, Jonathan	LB	Smith, Adrion	DB
Baker, Robert	WR	Annunziata, Sandy	OL	Fletcher, Michael	LB	Ivory, Clifford	DB
Palmer, Michael	WR	Landon, Jon	OL	O'Shea, Mike	LB	Younger, Jordan	DB
Avery, John	RB	St. John, Jude	OL	Eiben, Kevin	LB	Wheaton, Kenny	DB
Williams, John	RB	Feugill, John	OL	Mariuz, Ray	LB	Winters, Chuck	DB
Johnson, Jeff	RB	Williams, Bernard	OL	Bonner, Antonious	LB	Levingston, Bashir	KR
Allen, Damon	QB	Cantor, Noah	DL	Crumb, Mike	LB	Prefontaine, Noel	P/K

Logos

1914-59

1960-75

1976-88

1989-90

1991-93

1994

1995-2002

2003

2004

2005-

Contributors

Rick Matsumoto is a veteran reporter at the *Toronto Star* where he has waxed poetic about several sports, including Canadian football, over the past 35 years.

Jim O'Leary is a former Toronto sports columnist who now works in sports publishing and vintage photography through thesportgallery.com.

Jaime Stein contributes regularly to various CFL publications and was the voice of the Argos on AM640 Toronto Radio.

Photo Credits

The bulk of the photos in this book are courtesy of the Toronto Argonauts Football Club, with the exception of those noted below.

Canada's Sports Hall of Fame – Alexandra Studio/Turofsky: 14, 40, 42, 44 (right), 47 (top), 49 (bottom), 51, 56 (bottom), 60 (top), 61 (top), 62-63 (all), 64, 66-67 (all), 68 (top right), 69 (middle, bottom), 70-71, 72 (both), 74 (top), 75 (both), 77, 143 (top), front endpaper.

Canadian Football Hall of Fame and Museum: 20, 27, 29 (top), 35 (far left), 37, 38-39, 49 (top), 50 (both), 53 (top), 60 (bottom), 61 (bottom right), 73, 80, 83, 85 (right), 89.

Canadian Press: 19.

City of Toronto Archives: 47 (bottom).

Courtesy Charlie Camilleri: 54 (middle), 65 (top).

Courtesy David Gillen: 197.

Courtesy David S. Hunter: 88.

Courtesy David Watkins: 124-125.

Courtesy George F. McCauley: 22 (all), 25 (both), 27, 29 (bottom), 30 (both), 32, 33, 34, 35 (top), 44-45 (bottom), 52, 54 (top), 59, 61 (right).

Courtesy Ian Dunin-Markiewicz: 171, 192.

Courtesy Jaime Stein: 2, 9 (right), 188, 193 (bottom left, bottom right), 198 (middle right).

Courtesy Nick Turchiaro: 127 (middle, bottom), 130 (bottom), 131, 149 (all), 151 (top).

Courtesy Robert & Elizabeth Elliott: 35 (left).

Courtesy Zeke O'Connor: 74 (lower middle).

Dave Cheng: 194, 196, 203 (bottom), 204 (bottom right), 205 (top).

Harold Barkley Collection: 54 (bottom), 56 (top), 68 (lower right), 97 (bottom), 102 (top left), 102 (top), 103 (bottom right), 105 (bottom), 111 (left).

John Sokolowski: 193 (top), 194, 198 (top, bottom), 199, 200 (both), 201 (top), 202 (top), 203 (top), 204 (Fletcher, Wheaton, England), 204 (top, bottom left).

Michael Stuparyk / *Toronto Star*: 190.

All but one of the photographers stand their ground as the Alouettes take on the Argonauts, 1954.

Acknowledgements

Assembling an illustrated history of a franchise as storied as the Toronto Argonauts was a daunting task made possible only by the contributions and encouragement of many, whom the editors now wish to thank.

This book would not have happened without the unsung heroes dedicated to preserving Canada's sport history. We encountered these people at the Toronto Argonaut Rowing Club, the Canadian Football Hall of Fame, Canada's Sport Hall of Fame and the Toronto Archives. In every case they generously gave of their time and expertise.

George McCauley, a former Olympic rower and current Argonaut Rowing Club historian, enthusiastically contributed his vast knowledge of the rowing and football clubs, particularly with respect to the foundation of the Argos in 1873, as well as donating several historic photographs from his personal collection. George also introduced us to Bo Westlake, who kindly provided his essay on how the Grey Cup was saved after the 1947 fire that razed the Argonaut Rowing Club.

The Canadian Football Hall of Fame (footballhof.com) and Canada's Sport Hall of Fame (cshof.ca) are both afflicted by a shameful shortfall in funding. They owe their survival to people like John Cooper at the Football Hall of Fame, and Tanya Magnus and Sheryn Posen at the Sport Hall of Fame, who all deserve thanks for uncovering much of the stunning, early twentieth-century photography found in this book. Thanks, too, to the staff of the Toronto Archives.

The project MVP was Greg Oliver, whose research, writing, editing and layout skills are evident on every page of this book. Paul Hodgson is to be applauded for his bold page design, the dust jacket and overall artistic direction.

Considerable photography was contributed by the Toronto Argonauts, and the editors are grateful to Argos' front-office personnel Andrea Franklin, Eric Holmes, Beth Waldman and Jonathan Rubinoff. In addition, the editors are indebted to Jaime Stein, Nick Turchiaro, Dave Watkins, and Charlie Camilleri who provided photos from personal collections.

For the early history of Canadian football we thank Ian Speers for his research and writing about the birth and growth of pre-World War I football in Ontario. In particular, we benefited from these Speers essays: *Football at the University of Toronto, 1861–1880; Early Football in Ontario, 1880–1891*; and *The First Game of the Toronto Argonauts.* We also consulted the following essays: *The Toronto Argonauts to World War I*, by Robert Sproule; and *Historical Sketch of the Argonaut Rowing Club, 1872–1911*, by Henry O'Brien. Books consulted include: *The Argo Bounce* by Jay Teitel; *Legends of Autumn: The Glory Years of Canadian Football*, by Denny Boyd and Brian Scrivener; and *Football Today and Yesteryear* by Tony Allan.

We owe a huge thank you to an anonymous fan who faithfully brought his camera to Argo home games in the 1950s and '60s. The slides he created are the only Argo colour action photography we know of from this period. For help with photo identification we are grateful to several members of the Argo alumni who gather for a monthly luncheon. We crashed their party one afternoon and were kindly received by Don Durno, Zeke O'Connor, Nick Volpe, Charlie Camilleri, Bob Rumball, John Crinchich and Bill Lively.

Finally, our thanks to the many fans and former players who submitted their favourite Argo memory. This book's for you.